Marx's Theory of History

WILLIAM H. SHAW

Marx's Theory of History

STANFORD UNIVERSITY PRESS

Stanford, California

1978

Stanford University Press
Stanford, California
© 1978 by the Board of Trustees of the
Leland Stanford Junior University
Printed in the United States of America
ISBN 0-8047-0960-2
LC 77-76154

To My Parents

Acknowledgments

AN EARLIER VERSION of this essay was submitted as a dissertation to the London School of Economics and Political Science. I am grateful to them and to the Leverhulme Foundation for the financial support which allowed me to carry out the necessary research. My supervisor, John C. R. Charvet, also deserves my thanks for his helpful comments and his general support and assistance.

Far and away my greatest debt—one which it gives me pleasure to acknowledge—is to my friend and teacher, Gerald A. Cohen. His initial encouragement and generosity made this project possible, and his careful criticism and insight into historical materialism have improved it at every step. He has stimulated much that is sound in this essay, but I must emphasize that he will not agree with everything I have written, and that he is in no way responsible for my errors.

Finally, I would like to thank Mary Buckley for help which extended well beyond her proofreading of the manuscript.

W.H.S.

Contents

Marx's Theory of History

Introduction

THIS ESSAY is a contribution to the study of Karl Marx's theory of history.[1] Although the literature on Marx is rich, hardly any work deals with this particular subject in the systematic and sustained fashion which it requires. Understandably, most of the secondary sources, concerned with introducing the man and rehearsing his main ideas, do not approach the kind of analysis of Marx's theoretical commitments which is necessary if his conception of history is to be satisfactorily evaluated. Such works rarely offer more than a short chapter on historical materialism, and usually limit themselves to paraphrasing the "Author's Preface" to *A Contribution to the Critique of Political Economy*. On the other hand, more detailed and erudite investigations, centering on contemporary debates, have focused their attentions elsewhere; studies have ranged over Marx's economics, dialectics, theory of alienation, and intellectual evolution, but insufficient effort has been directed toward historical materialism.

The prevailing consensus among scholars suggests that the meaning of Marx's theory of history is unclear. The various accounts of it are not all mutually compatible, and many are marred by incompleteness and inaccuracy. In general, Marx's thought is the subject of vigorous disputation, and there is a maze of conflicting authority. Marx himself is not entirely responsible for this state of affairs. For while the study of Marx has grown more sophisticated over the years, high standards of scholarship have not always been maintained, and a slackness persists which one imagines would not be tolerated in other fields. The complex causes of this need not be sought here, but Marx has clearly been difficult to examine dispassionately. The requirements of the book trade have, in addition, encouraged rather one-sided, "novel" treatments of Marx. In any case, where patient examination has been required, individual flights of fancy have been indulged; where reasoned and close exegesis has been needed, textual infidelity has triumphed.

Before commenting on the specific problems with which I shall be concerned, a few points must be made to avoid confusion about the nature of this project. Although I handle the theory sympathetically, my intention is not to defend it or revise it; rather, I attempt to excavate what Marx's theory says, unpack its meaning, explore its nuances, and highlight some of its internal difficulties. I treat historical materialism, basically, as an empirical, scientific theory (or as an attempt to be such a theory). This is the way, I believe, that Marx himself understood it.

This might be thought to beg the question: Was Marx actually doing what he thought he was doing? That is, it is possible that while Marx claimed or actually believed himself to be offering a scientific theory of history, he was in fact only putting window dressing on some metaphysical views. For instance, some secularized version of Judaeo-Christian eschatology or a normative theory of alienation might be thought to underlie historical materialism.

While the materialist conception of history may well have resided in Marx's head alongside of a variety of ethical and other commitments, I cannot accept the position that historical materialism must be understood or evaluated only in terms of some supposed philosophical framework. Although Marx's theory raises certain philosophical issues, I do not believe it profitable to see the theory as derived from some imputed metaphysic. However, it is not part of my thesis to demonstrate that the Marx of "scientific" historical materialism is the "real" Marx. There is certainly an empirical side to Marx—he and most of his followers have thought so—and it is this with which I shall deal. Since one cannot really deny that Marx does appear to offer such a theory (the controversial question is whether it is really the most fundamental aspect of Marx's thought), it is legitimate, and I believe important, to explore the theory within its own frame of reference. Similarly, one may find it valuable to examine *Capital*, if one wishes, strictly as an economics text.

An apparently empirical theory can (and indeed must) be appraised apart from its metaphysical backdrop or its author's nonempirical beliefs. If the theory is scientifically untenable, its philosophical embodiment makes no difference: a good metaphysic cannot compensate for a bad empirical theory. On the other hand, if the theory (or parts of it) were to be found scientifically fruitful, it could be dissociated from its philosophical base. In treating historical materialism as an empirical theory (since this is the fashion in which Marx tenders it), I admittedly abstract it from other significant and engaging aspects of Marx's perspective. For example, his "scientific" vision of the evolution of man's social relations in response to expanding productive capacity also conveys the more "spiritual" story of man's alienation in class society from his true social being, which is to be realized in the communist future. Insofar as this second meaning is built into Marx's conception of history, though, what one makes of it will be influenced by one's evaluation of historical materialism as a scientific theory.

Of course, the danger is that Marx's thought may be misrepresented: that is, that one will take it to be essentially economic or social-scientific when in fact Marx was attempting something else. The reader may well feel that crucial features of Marx are neglected when *Capital* is treated as only an economics treatise, or when, as in this book, his theory of history is divorced from his apparently normative beliefs or from his theory of alienation. Nevertheless, what I intend to offer is an analysis of one portion of the empirical side of Marx's thought. The fact that this side has traditionally been taken to be that which is distinctive of

Marx may enhance this essay, but my study is not undermined if such a "scientific" conception of Marx turns out to be misguided.

Few others have attended closely enough to historical materialism, and that is good reason for sticking to the topic at hand—rather than undertaking yet another ambitious, all-encompassing treatise on Marx. It is this gap in the literature which I hope to fill partially myself and to encourage others to work on. I shall not, however, discuss the whole of Marx's thinking on history; rather, I treat only one aspect of it. I am concerned with Marx's general infrastructural model of historical change, with the elements that provide history's unity and push it forward. That is, I deal with the economic dynamic, the interplay of productive forces and relations of production, which Marx understood to underlie historical change and evolution. This theme is important precisely because historical materialism itself assigns explanatory primacy to this particular dynamic. Though the theory directs one's attention to this nexus, among students of Marx there is neither concurrence about the meaning of the basic terms involved nor agreement about the manner in which history's fundamental momentum is provided.

While the territory to be investigated here is not large, it is nevertheless crucial ground for the reconstruction of Marx's theory of history. It would not be too misleading to see this entire essay as a struggle to elucidate a portion of that dense statement by Marx of his own view in the "Preface" to *The Critique of Political Economy*. I undertake to sift more finely than has hitherto been attempted two central concepts of Marx's theory, to unravel the evolutionary dynamic which is basic to Marx's perspective, and to trace its operation through the specifics of both Marx's analysis of capitalism and his reflections on precapitalist history. What is necessary is careful exegesis and a more even-handed presentation of Marx's theory, one which does not omit its lacunae and inconsistencies; this I aim to provide.

Chapter One probes the concepts of Produktivkräfte and

Produktionsverhältnisse. By means of textual analysis, their meaning for Marx is fully explicated, and they are assigned a place within his larger perception of society. Further, it is argued that these concepts are neither incoherent nor inconsistent, as some have supposed. On this basis, Chapter Two delineates the character of Marx's historical theory and defends its basic intelligibility. Unlike most contemporary exponents of Marx, I champion a technological-determinist interpretation.

The next two chapters show how Marx envisioned his dialectic as clothed in history. Chapter Three depicts the transition from capitalism to socialism in terms of my previous discussion. How this transformation is actuated by a conflict between the forces and relations of production is revealed, and this account is then connected with the role played in Marx's thought by the proletariat and by dialectics. Chapter Four traces Marx's grasp of the evolutionary course of pre-capitalist history. While indicating the limits of Marx's insight, this treatment allows for a more accurate understanding of his general perspective. Marx was a student of history, but his comprehension of its actual path has not previously been surveyed with a close enough eye to his theoretical commitments.

Chapter Five reviews some of the problems with Marx's productive-force determinism, and concludes with some reflections on the scientific evaluation of his legacy. In such a fashion, then, the basic contours of Marx's historical materialism may be more sharply delineated and our command of it strengthened.

I do not exhaust the subject of historical materialism, but I do claim to present, accurately and scrupulously, the core of that theory and to show how Marx interpreted history in terms of it; to my knowledge this has never been accomplished. As intimated above, I maintain a "deterministic" interpretation of his theory, which credits the forces of production with the determining role in history, and I attempt to illuminate more precisely the primacy of the productive forces and their explanatory role within historical materialism. Such a version of Marx seems to have enjoyed currency among Marx's early and "orthodox" followers (notably Plekhanov), although they never subjected the theory to close enough critical scrutiny.

Most contemporary writers, however, are unhappy with such an old-fashioned, deterministic, and evolutionary rendering of Marx. Commentators of all stripes agree on its vulgarity, and each in his own way has sought to make Marx's theory less contentious and more palatable. Despite the sophistication of this work, the price has generally been a less accurate—and less interesting—account of Marx's theory of history. What I reprove such interpreters for, then, is their method of delivering Marx from his critics. To concede, for instance, that the notion of a determining factor in history is incoherent and then to argue that Marx must have something else in view is to kill Marx with kindness. Marx was surely concerned to say more than simply that the economic base is important, or that everything is related to everything. Since I will later be trying to show exactly to what Marx's theory commits him, I need not expand on this here. I only announce that I will be offering a more "fundamentalist" interpretation of Marx than many friends of Marx have felt comfortable defending.[2] But by simultaneously showing the extent to which Marx's theory of history can be upheld against his critics, I believe that I have done him no disservice.

Before going on, a few procedural comments must be made. First, this essay does not enter into the debate about the relation between the "young" and the "old" Marx—in what sense(s) they are disparate or consonant, and which represents the "real" Marx. Historical materialism, as it was evolved around the time of *The German Ideology* and subsequently elaborated, is the province of Marx's mature thought; generally speaking, I shall not be concerned with earlier adumbrations of this theory. Nor do I examine the development of Marx's materialist conception. Changes in Marx's ideas are noted where they are germane, but I do not offer an intellectual biography.

Secondly, I am concerned with Marx's own theory of history

and not with later interpretations of it, except insofar as these are relevant to the comprehension of Marx's own position. Marx's intellectual relation with Engels is complex and deserves separate study. While I am cognizant of their different tastes and abilities, I find no systematic divergences between them in the subject under consideration. On some points Engels' authority constitutes the only guide to Marx's thought, but Engels' statements are not necessarily Marx's burdens, and I strive to employ Engels' evidence judiciously.

Finally, I am occasionally obliged to quote extensively from Marx, both to document my own interpretation and to allow my points to be expounded through Marx's own words. I endeavor to render Marx as being uniform and clear whenever this is possible without violating his meaning; frequently, I make this effort by defending him against a critic or a misguided votary.

CHAPTER ONE

The Anatomy of Production

IN 1857, in a rough manuscript intended to introduce the *Grundrisse*, Marx included the following statement in a list of points to be kept in mind: "5. *Dialectic of the concepts productive force (means of production) and relation of production*, the limits of *this dialectical* connection, which does not abolish the real differences, have to be defined."[1] Unfortunately, Marx never really proceeded to expand upon this note by explicating his conception of "productive forces" and "relations of production." This deficiency is striking: although these two concepts constitute the centerpiece of historical materialism, they are rarely wielded with precision, even by those who embrace this theory. Still, Marx's writings do unfold the "dialectic" of these two concepts, and this chapter proposes to go some way toward elucidating them. This labor should lay the foundation for the reconstruction, in later chapters, of Marx's model of historical change as it applies to the transformation of specific social formations. This, in turn, should provide a fuller and more accurate specification of the core of the materialist theory of history than has heretofore been offered.

It has become rather fashionable to blame Marx for failing to outline clearly his concepts for us (and his sympathizers have advanced many excuses on his behalf for this), but although

Marx did not always employ his concepts as deftly as one might wish, this point has been greatly overstated. Bertell Ollman, to take an extreme example, believes that if Marx means what common sense and ordinary language suggest he means, then "Marx is not only guilty of ridiculous exaggeration but of a gross ignorance of history and the simplest facts of economic life."[2] Marx, it appears, did not use his words in anything like the mundane way in which most mortals do; accordingly, Ollman dedicates himself to the unenviable task of excavating what Marx really had in mind, but was apparently unable to state.

A principle underlying this essay is that, generally speaking, Marx means what he says: there is no need to explain this in terms of some alleged "underlying" philosophy or a unique use of words. I do not claim that there are no ambiguities, discrepancies, puzzles, or plain mistakes in Marx; I merely contend that with some effort Marx's ideas can be made reasonably consistent and coherent—or, where that is not possible, that the problems in them can at least be identified. Difficulties in examining the content and interrelation of the above-mentioned concepts do not result from Marx's language per se, but rather because the concepts themselves are so basic to his theoretical perspective. They are of the essence of Marx's conception of society; as a result, their consistent and full explication takes time and care.

To adequately grasp historical materialism, one must understand its conceptual furniture. The concepts "productive forces" and "relations of production" are fundamental to Marx's perception of history—in particular, to his view of the dynamics of historical change and social evolution. Their clarification is a necessary task. Because of the importance of getting a handle on these notions, and because of the confused way in which they are frequently conceived, I am obliged to proceed slowly and with thorough documentation. Still, I do not claim to be able to prove my definitions, although I maintain that they more comfortably accord with Marx's usage and overall intentions than any rival interpretation. With a thinker as complex and fecund as Marx, it is not always possible to give incontrovertible and rigid meanings to his terms, and in any case one cannot suppose that this could be accomplished by narrow textual discussion alone—without reference to his purpose in employing his concepts and to their role within his theory.

The fact that both of the concepts which this chapter examines can be made intelligible and consistent is the reason for rebuking commentators like Ollman for yielding the field so quickly to Marx's critics: there is no need to plead a special case for Marx's use of words when his concepts are coherent. I hope also to show that they are not so intractable.

Productive Forces

Productive forces are those elements which are both basic and essential to the production process, not in the wide sense of including all activities or factors which are necessary for society to carry on production, but in the narrower sense of the simple factors of the labor process—that is, those elements which analysis reveals as part of the immediate production process itself. The labor process is the process of producing material use-values. With the help of instruments, man's activity effects an alteration, designed from commencement, on the material worked: a product results. Any labor process involves labor-power and means of production; these elements will be seen to constitute what Marx understands as the "productive forces."

Means of Production

The means of production (Produktionsmittel) are identified by Marx as the material factors of production,[3] the objective conditions of labor,[4] and labor's material and means; they are indispensable for its "realization."[5] Marx declares that both the instruments of labor (Arbeitsmittel) and the object of labor (Arbeitsgegenstand) are "means of production,"[6] noting the apparent paradox that uncaught fish are thus means of production in the fishing industry.* "The means of production in every labor-process, regardless of the social conditions in which it takes place, are divided into instruments and objects of labor."[7]

That part of the means of production which Marx designates as Arbeitsmittel is usually translated as "instruments of labor," but it should be understood as the "means of labor" in a wide sense, embracing all objects necessary for carrying on the labor-process—workshops, canals, roads, and even the earth's soil itself.[8] The means of labor may be mobile or immobile:

A part of the instruments of labor [Arbeitsmittel], which includes the general conditions of labor, is either localized as soon as it enters the process of production as an instrument of labor, i.e., is prepared for its productive function, such as for instance machinery, or is produced from the outset in its immovable, localized form, such as improvements of the soil, factory buildings, blast furnaces, canals, railways, etc. . . . On the other hand an instrument of labor may physically change continually from place to place, may move about, and nevertheless be constantly in the process of production; for instance, a locomotive, a ship, beasts of burden, etc.[9]

Instruments of labor in the more restricted sense of tools are, thus, only a subset of the class of Arbeitsmittel.

"The material forms of existence of constant capital, the means of production, do not however consist only of such instruments of labor but also of materials of labor in various stages of processing, and of auxiliary materials."[10] The other part of the means of production is the object of labor or, as Marx sometimes refers to it, the material upon which labor works: "In the actual labor process [the laborer] *utilizes* the means of labor as the conductor of his labor and the object of labor as the material in which his labor manifests itself."[11]

Prima facie, the distinction is that the objects of labor, including raw materials and auxiliary substances, lose their characteris-

Capital 1: 181n (*Werke* 23: 196n). Elsewhere, Marx suggests that water, too, is an element of the labor process in fishing. *Theories of Surplus Value* 2: 21. In this regard, it is worth observing that the terms discussed in this section, as well as the concept "productive forces" itself, are terms of art; one should not allow their ordinary connotations to obscure their technical meaning for Marx.

tic form when inserted in the labor process, while the instruments of labor—such as tools, machines, and workshops—are of use in the labor process only so long as they retain their original shape.[12] Further, some objects of labor may enter physically into the product itself; by contrast, the instruments of labor, which help to create the use-value, do not become part of it. However, Marx finds that the means of transportation are an exception to this rule.[13] His ratiocination is that the use-value created by employing means of transportation—unlike other means of labor—is instantaneously consumed; but generally speaking, the Arbeitsmittel cannot enter into the produced use-value in the same manner as raw materials do: they are productively consumed but not consumed as part of the product.

With reference to the Arbeitsgegenstände, Marx discriminates between (1) the objects of labor provided spontaneously by nature, such as fish, timber, or mineral wealth, and (2) the objects of labor which have been filtered through previous human labor; only the latter are "raw materials." "All raw material is the object of labor, but not every object of labor is raw material."[14] In the *Grundrisse* Marx, arguably, uses Rohstoff and Rohmaterial to capture the distinction between (1) and (2) above.[15] This contrast is also reflected in the difference between extractive industry and manufacturing industry. While the former would obviously ply some objects filtered through human labor, essentially it labors on (1). Manufacturing industry, on the other hand, generally utilizes (2) only.

Raw materials, strictly speaking then, may be either the principal substance of the product or an accessory, such as coal, oil, hay, dye, or chlorine, although at times Marx appears to identify "raw materials" with the principal substance itself.[16] The principal raw material is worked directly into the product, while auxiliary materials (Hilfsstoffe) are either consumed immediately by the instruments of labor or are mixed with the principal raw material to modify it. This difference, which appears to hinge on the nature of the labor process's consumption of the raw material, disappears, Marx tells us, in chemical industries, since no type of raw material used therein retains its original composition.[17]

Similarly, the division between instruments of labor and objects of labor is acknowledged by Marx to be far from rigid.[18] Further, if a distinction can be ascertained between particular means and objects of labor in one labor process, it may not hold in another. Possessing various properties, an object can have many uses. It may serve as a raw material in very different processes; it may be both an instrument and a raw material; or it may even (like coal in coal mining) be both the product of, and the means of production in, the same operation.[19]

Despite the rather intuitive level of Marx's discussion and the qualifications above, I would suggest that in any particular labor process those things with which, and on which, labor-power is exercised could be recognized. The range of items which Marx includes within Arbeitsmittel suggests that in doubtful cases the presumption should be in favor of interpreting "means of production" in a wide sense. The productive forces are simply those elements which are utilized (or at least eligible to be employed) in the immediate production process. They may well have other (even simultaneous) functions in addition to their role in production: canals and roads are more than means of production in the transport industry.

Finally, I emphasize that there is no license in Marx's texts to incorporate within the "productive forces" those things—such as morality or the judiciary—which may be necessary for production to continue; the term is restricted to those elements which can actually be utilized in the labor process. The distinction is between those things which occasion production or permit it to proceed and those things which are physically part of, and materially necessary for, production. Only the latter may be productive forces.

Labor-power

There is really no doubt that Marx reckoned labor-power within the "productive forces." It is a mistake to conceive the means of production—the material conditions of production—as the "productive forces" apart from the most important element of production.* The productive forces are frequently referred to, by Marx, as "die Produktivkräfte *der Arbeit.*" Labor either creates the means of production or appropriates them in the labor process. At the same time, the skill and knowledge of labor develop. The means of production are, to a large extent, only the material manifestations of labor's productive capacities. "Nature builds no machines, no locomotives, railways, electric telegraphs, self-acting mules etc. These are products of human industry; natural material transformed into organs of the human will over nature, or of human participation in nature. They are *organs of the human brain, created by the human hand*; the power of knowledge, objectified."[20] The productive forces of labor encompass not only the material means of production which enable labor to produce but the powers of labor-power itself: skill, training, know-how, experience. Indeed, "Arbeitskraft" looks like a species of "Produktivkraft." In line with this, Marx refers to the "development of the material (and therefore also of the mental) productive forces."[21] Labor-power is a productive force, one which develops greatly with the introduction of wage-labor and, as a consequence of this, disciplined and coordinated production.[22]

Karl Korsch, although he does not deny this, goes to another extreme: his *Karl Marx* includes among the productive forces not only labor-power but the revolutionary proletariat, because, reasons Korsch, it is the workers who by their revolutionary action set free the forces potentially existing in social labor.[23] This notion originates from Marx's comment that: "Of all the instruments of production, the greatest productive power is the revolutionary class itself." A glance at the entire passage from which

*Plekhanov, for one example, commits this error in *The Development of the Monist View of History*, pp. 124–25. There are, however, places in which both Marx and Engels employ "productive forces" in a manner which seems synonymous with "means of production"—for example, *Selected Works* 1: 160, and 3: 145—although it is unclear whether they were expanding "means of production" or contracting "productive forces." In any event, such passages—while harmless in their context—do represent lapses in rigor. Neither Marx nor Engels was as meticulous as one might wish with the concepts of historical materialism.

this sentence comes reveals how risky it would be to hang such an interpretation of "productive forces" on it alone:

> For the oppressed class to be able to emancipate itself it is necessary that the productive powers already acquired and the existing social relations should no longer be capable of existing side by side. Of all the instruments of production, the greatest productive power is the revolutionary class itself. The organization of revolutionary elements as a class supposes the existence of all the productive forces which could be engendered in the bosom of the old society.[24]

Although the labor-power of the proletariat is an important part of the productive forces, Marx's reference to the class itself is hyperbolic: otherwise, the revolutionary class could not come into existence until it already existed (since it would be part of the productive forces which its existence presupposes). Elsewhere Marx makes it clear that the revolutionary class is not to be confused with the productive forces—in a strict sense—which prepare its arrival. Thus *The German Ideology* refers to the "material elements of a complete revolution . . . namely, on the one hand the existing productive forces, on the other the formation of a revolutionary mass."[25]

In a later chapter I shall discuss this issue in connection with the transition from capitalism to socialism, but I put it aside now in order to return to the examination of labor-power. In *Capital*, Marx advances his definition of labor-power: "By labor-power or capacity for labor [Arbeitsvermögen] is to be understood the aggregate of those mental and physical capabilities existing in a human being, which he exercises whenever he produces a use-value of any description."[26] The labor process, Marx tells us, is human action with a view to the production of material use-values. It is the consumption of labor-power. Labor-power, on the contrary, exists only as a capacity or power of the living individual; but by working, the bearer of labor-power becomes in reality what, previously, he was only potentially: labor-power in action, a laborer.* "Man himself, viewed as the impersonation [Dasein] of labor-power, is a natural object, a thing, although a

---

Capital 1: 171, 177 (*Werke* 23: 185, 192). Labor power, writes Marx at *Capital* 1: 538 (*Werke* 23: 561), "is as different from its function, labor, as a machine is from the work it performs."

living conscious thing, and labor is the manifestation of this power residing in him."[27] Labor-power itself is energy transferred to a human organism by means of "nourishing matter."

Although Marx refers in *Capital* to labor itself as one of the elementary "Momente" of the labor process,[28] he is usually found discussing labor-power (or sometimes the laborer) as constituting one of the two basic factors (Faktoren) of production, regardless of its social form.[29] The Moore-Aveling edition of *Capital* translates Momente, in the passage alluded to above, as "factors," although it could probably be more accurately rendered as "aspects," "moments," or "instances" in a slightly Hegelian sense. This is no mere verbal quibble because the distinction between Momente and Faktoren enables this question to be answered: Which is part of the productive forces, Arbeit or Arbeitskraft? Labor itself is an abstract aspect of any labor process, while labor-power is one of the elements which has to be combined for such a production process to occur. Laboring actually constitutes production; unlike labor-power, it is not something used in production. While this difference might appear oversubtle to the modern reader, for Marx the distinction was far from scholastic since it contained the key to the riddle of surplus-value. Labor-power is the capacity to labor, and labor is, in turn, the manifestation of this power. Labor-power has the ability to develop, to gain skill, and to become more experienced, which its mere expenditure, labor itself, lacks. For this reason, labor-power, not labor, is a productive force. It is labor-power which is the carrier of the skills and experience, developed through time, of mankind. "Since there are always several generations of laborers living at one time, and working together at the manufacture of a given article, the technical skill, the tricks of the trade thus acquired, become established, and are accumulated and handed down."[30]

Here, Marx is discussing manufacture proper, but his point is more general. When, as in *The German Ideology*, he mentions the "productive forces handed down to [each generation] by all preceding generations," this does not refer to the means of production alone.[31] *Capital* makes this clear: "The reproduction of the working-class carries with it the accumulation of skill, that is handed down from one generation to another."[32] Labor-power furnishes the productive forces with their continuity through the historical process. The instruments of man's production may supply the fossils which allow the story of his developing productive capacity as well as of the various stages in his social and economic organization to be unfolded, but it is labor-power which provides the connection between those fossils. The conditioning of man's relations of production by the development of his productive forces is one of the dominant themes of historical materialism. Central to this, and thus to the coherence of history, is the development of labor-power.[33] Thus labor-power can hardly be excluded from the "productive forces."

Although men are the bearers of labor-power, it is the labor-power and not the men which belongs to the productive forces. This is despite the fact that it is only through men that labor-power enters into the production process. Men are more than labor-powers. They stand in relations other than production (although they are only able to subsist because of production). Since this is the case, Marx is able to indict capitalism for turning laborers into the mere appendages of capital, for which they exist simply as labor-power.[34] Similarly, when Marx says the development of the productive forces may be at the expense of human beings,[35] the productive forces include the laborer's own labor-power, his productive activity which is under the alien control of capital. It is precisely because the productive forces *do* subsume labor-power that "alienation," as discussed by Marx in his famous *1844 Manuscripts*, continues in a relevant sense as a motif in Marx's mature works.

The distinction between a laborer and his labor-power raises the question of the status of those things—in particular, food and clothing—which are necessary to the worker's life: are they productive forces? Although an unfed laborer can supply, at best, only diminished labor-power, this does not mean that the "means of subsistence" are part of the "productive forces," because the latter are defined as the elements of production. To include within the productive forces those things which are necessary to the production of either labor-power or the means of production would be to open the door to an infinite regression. Marx is very clear that the "means of subsistence constitute no element of the production process."[36] In the *Grundrisse*, he writes: "The worker's *approvisionnement* arises out of the production process, as product, as result; but it never enters as such into the production process, because it is a finished product for individual consumption, enters directly into the worker's consumption, and is exchanged for [wages]."[37] The "productive forces" are defined not just as those things which are necessary for production—since many things like laws or soldiers might be necessary for production to be successfully continued—but as those things which are the basic elements of the actual labor process, those factors which are used in this process.

This reasoning is accurate with regard to food, but the situation is slightly different with regard to clothing. Some of the laborer's clothing functions to preserve his labor-power (as food does) or to satisfy certain social mores, but it may also be necessitated by the nature of the work process. Often, in fact, clothing is part of the equipment supplied by the capitalist. Articles like face-masks, helmets, protective vests, and shoes would seem to be among the means of production in certain labor procedures, and it is arguable that all the other clothing which the laborer must wear for protection while working is one of the materially necessary components of the work process and is thus part of the productive forces.

Labor-power is of no use without means of production, and changes in labor-power are obviously bound up with the improvement of production. On the one hand, new instruments do not come into existence simply because other new implements are available to manufacture them; more knowledgeable labor-power is necessary to create them. Although it may be equipped with new means of labor, labor-power itself is still, in this situation, the key Produktivkraft. On the other hand, the introduction of any invention requires laborers skilled enough to employ it. If they are lacking, the development of production which the invention's utilization would otherwise promote will be restrained: "The inventions of Vaucanson, Arkwright, Watt, and others, were, however, practicable, only because those inventors found, ready to hand, a considerable number of skilled mechanical workmen, placed at their disposal by the manufacturing period."[38]

Of course the introduction of a new tool, instead of necessitating more skilled labor-power, may permit less talented laborers to perform the same work. This obviously characterized the general transition from production by handicraft or manufacture to that under modern industry. Productivity—the output in a given time with a given expenditure of labor-power—grew at the expense of the quality of the majority of the employed labor-power. This is consistent with Marx's usage when, for example, he writes that "in order to make the collective laborer, and through him capital, rich in social productive power [Produktivkraft], each individual must be made poor in individual productive powers [an individuellen Produktivkräften]."[39]

This helps to clarify *The German Ideology*'s discussion of the universal character of the proletariat's appropriation of the productive forces: "The appropriation of these forces is itself nothing more than the development of the individual capacities corresponding to the material instruments of production. The appropriation of a totality of instruments of production is, for this reason, the development of a totality of capacities in the individuals themselves."[40] Here "appropriation" equivocates. While Marx was later to stress that modern industry itself technically requires that the productive powers of each individual be enriched—that is, that it necessitates "variation of labor, fluency of function, universal mobility of the laborer"—this is not the claim registered by this passage.[41] Here, society's labor-power as a whole expands as it appropriates the modern means of production, in the sense of actually producing use-values, but this advance demands that social control end the anarchy of capitalist production. It leads, in other words, to the legal and political expropriation of the means of production by the proletariat, and it is this event which allows for the full blossoming of the "totality of capacities in the individuals themselves."

Marx's continuing concern with this theme manifests itself in the *Critique of the Gotha Program*, where he talks about that higher stage of communist society "after the productive forces have also increased with the all-round development of the individual, and all the springs of cooperative wealth flow more abundantly."[42] The development of the individual requires both the development and control—in common with others—of social production and, hence, the development and control of his own labor-power: something much different from the preservation of narrow craft skill. This holds regardless of whether one finds *Capital* Volume Three's contrast of the realm of freedom with the realm of necessity to conflict with the glowing picture of the nature of socialist labor offered by Marx's early works.*

Science and Cooperation

It follows from what has been said so far about the nature of labor-power that scientific and technological knowledge is an attribute of it. Because technology is an important part of modern industry, M. M. Bober, for example, in his essay on Marx's theory of history, treats science as a productive force, but sees this as a problem: "Marx intends to offer a materialistic conception of history. Yet he frequently stresses the power of science as a component of modern technique and production. The incorporation of science in the foundation of his theory is no more defensible than the inclusion of all other nonmaterial phenomena."[43]

Several issues are intertwined here, but science does not really

---

*Compare *Capital* 3: 820, with that famous passage in *The German Ideology* (*Selected Works* 1: 36) which looks forward to the time when it will be "possible for me to do one thing today and another tomorrow, to hunt in the morning, fish in the afternoon, rear cattle in the evening, criticize after dinner, just as I have a mind, without ever becoming hunter, fisherman, shepherd, or critic."

pose a radically new problem for Marx's conception of the productive forces. Any labor process involves conscious agents; their consciousness, along with their skill, experience, and know-how, is part of the labor-power which is engaged in producing use-values. Scientific and technical knowledge simply represents labor-power of a higher order. Science cannot enter production except by means of an agent, although this is often belied by our use of language: for example, casual talk about the application of science to industry sounds as if science were just a different item among the means of production, as if it were applied to industry just like electrical power or a system of machinery. To oust science from the productive forces in the name of materialism is both foolish and misguided: it supposes that Marx could offer a materialist conception of history only if material production itself were devoid of consciousness. "But the *development of science* . . . is only one aspect, one form in which the *development of the human productive forces*, i.e., of wealth, appears."[44]

The issues which have confused this point are not hard to recognize. First is the fact that there are scientists pursuing scientific research separate and distinct from actual material production. Second is that scientific knowledge constitutes a corpus outside of whatever application to production it may have, an intellectual structure which while resembling ideologies like philosophy or religion has an endurance and claim to truth regardless of the nature of the society from which it emanates. These two points are not conjured away by a Marxist demonstration of the functional need of capitalist production for more and more advanced scientific research or of the contamination of science by the ideology of the era, interesting as these displays might be in their own right. Scientific knowledge is at least in part autonomous from the production process and its needs. The labor of the scientist does not usually add value to commodities, and to some extent, capitalist production receives the advantages of scientific advance gratuitously. These benefits are the fruits of "new developments of the universal labor [allegemeinen Arbeit des menschlichen Geistes] of the human spirit and their social application through combined labor."[45] Capital is in a position to monopolize all such advances of human knowledge: "Capital is . . . the absorber and appropriator . . . of the general social productive forces, such as science."[46]

This leads to a third issue which obfuscates the relation of science to the productive forces. A fundamental feature of a worker's alienation is the fact that capital comes to embody the intellectual powers of production as an alien force over and against him; since the process of production is completely out of his control, the growing power, authority, and intelligence of capital represent loss of those qualities for the individual worker. This development "is completed in modern industry, which makes science a productive force [Produktionspotenz] distinct from labor and presses it into the service of capital."[47] "Potenz" means power, and Marx is employing a different expression here from "Produktivkräfte" (productive forces), so he may not have equated the two. In any event, Marx is speaking rather figuratively: science does heighten the power of production, but it is not a power which is distinct from labor-power in the same sense as the means of production could be said to be distinct. The intelligence which presides over the process still manifests itself in agents of that process—if not in the simple and routine toil of the average laborer, then in the work of the technicians or overseers of production. Although workers in capitalism lack a command over both their day-to-day work and society's production in general, which Marx thought they would regain under socialism, Marx held that there is a work of control which is required by the large-scale and cooperative nature of production and which is independent of the control necessitated by its capitalist character (with the accompanying antagonism of interest between labor and capital).[48] This supervision, which involves the scientific management of the entire production process and in a sense embodies science or technology within it, would remain even in a cooperatively run factory.

The relation of science to the productive process is further intertwined with two other factors: the introduction and employment of natural forces, and the social character of cooperative labor.

> Apart from the natural substances, it is possible to incorporate in the productive process natural forces, which do not cost anything, to act as agents with more or less heightened effect. The degree of their effectiveness depends on methods and scientific developments which cost the capitalist nothing.
> The same is true of the social combination of labor-power in the process of production and of the accumulated skill of the individual laborers.[49]

Marx makes clear that the utilization of natural forces does not add value to the product in addition to that of the already employed labor-power and complementary means of production, although the utilization of natural forces surely increases the productivity of man's labor (and may thus lower the value of a commodity). Cooperation in the production process, which constitutes the fundamental form of capitalist production, presents a parallel phenomenon. The simultaneous employment of many individuals in similar, consecutive, or reciprocative tasks lends their collective production a power or productiveness which is not reducible to the expenditure of so much individual, isolated labor. This is one of the most important levers for amplifying man's productive power in general—it is also one which, like science, appears to be purely an attribute of capital, one of its inherent properties.[50]

Large scale cooperation is what gives labor its social character. The total labor process combines many workers who collectively produce a single product. Although the whole process may be scientific, this is not true for each individual labor-power. Some work with their hands, others with their heads: "the one as manager, engineer, technician, etc.; the other as overseer; the third, as a direct hand laborer or a simple handyman."[51] The whole process of capitalist production is cooperative and scientific, but the process of cooperation and a scientific ordering of production are not elements used in production; rather, they are an organization or relation of production, a way of producing. The principles of scientific management which dictate cooperative organization, however, are part of the labor-power of certain agents in the production process, and in this way they are part of the productive forces.[52]

Cooperation expands productive efficiency but is not itself a productive force. On this point commentators have been mislead by a certain equivocalness in Marx's language. While Produktivität is commonly used by him to refer to productivity, Marx also utilizes Produktivkraft to carry the same meaning, as in his reference to "the increase in the productive power [Produktivkraft] of labor through cooperation, division of labor, machinery, etc."[53] The two senses of Produktivkraft (or -kräfte) are displayed in this remark from the third volume of *Capital*: "The development of the social productiveness [Produktivkraft] of labor is manifested in . . . the magnitude of the already produced productive forces [Produktivkräfte]."[54]

This use of Produktivkraft, both for productive power and for that which has productive power, parallels Marx's dual use of use-value and exchange-value both for attributes of objects and for objects having those attributes.[55] Not only is productive power or productiveness an attribute of each of the individual factors of production which constitute the "productive forces," it is also an attribute of the process of production as a whole, of society's general productive capacity. Obviously there is a close connection between the notions of "productive forces" and "productivity." To speak of the productive forces developing is to suggest that the productivity of production—the goods produced by a given input of immediate labor—is increasing; similarly, decreasing productivity may signal a decline in society's productive forces. Of course, the concepts are discrete, and productivity can be enhanced, for example, by the reorganization of existing productive forces rather than by the introduction of new ones.

Two Objections Examined

Against the rather traditional interpretation defended by this essay, it has been maintained that the "productive forces" are not things at all, but rather a relation of production. According to the Althusserian school, through which this view has become influential, the productive forces should be conceived as a certain type of connection within the mode of production, namely, the real appropriation of nature, or "the technical relations of production."[56] The productive forces in this view are not the elements of production *tout court*, but the system of relations of these factors in the actual production process.

While no positive textual evidence has ever been adduced by proponents of this position on its behalf, it is favored by them over the view endorsed here because that interpretation is held (1) to be too abstract, (2) to accord ill with the proper conception of the relations of production (which is thought *not* to include both the technical organization of production and its property or socioeconomic arrangement), and (3) to open the door to some sort of technological-determinist reading of Marx.[57] With regard to (1), it is hard to see why the abstractness of the present definition of productive forces should weigh against it; no one claims that this definition, *qua* definition, reveals anything at all about specific historical modes of production—indeed, how could a definition do this? Further, the types of connection which the opposing view identifies as the "productive forces" seem just as "eternal to production" and "abstract."[58] As for (2), in the second part of this chapter I shall document the fact that the term "relations of production," as wielded by Marx, embraces both types of relations mentioned above. Here I only suggest that far from it being infelicitous to classify the actual relations in the production process under "relations of production," this would seem to be implied by the term itself. Claim (3), however, I do not dispute, because this essay defends just such an interpretation of Marx.

This attempt to collapse the distinction between the productive forces and their technical organization in production clashes with Marx's and Engels' frequent use of "productive forces" in a manner which suggests that they have in mind the factors of production which I have described as the productive forces. They speak of the already produced productive forces and the objectification of the productive forces,[59] and call machinery a productive force.[60] They refer to "the sum of the productive forces" and treat labor-power, in one passage, as units of the productive forces.[61] Marx and Engels often talk about the ownership of the productive forces or about their being idled or underemployed (say by crisis)—remarks which do not suggest that the productive forces are actually relations. Further, Marx explicitly distinguishes the productive forces of labor from the particular forms of labor—for example, cooperation, manufacture, or the factory.[62] These social forms are relations,[63] but these relations are not to be identified with the productive forces which they involve. Fundamental to Marx's theory is the possibility of distinguishing between the productive forces and both their technical and social organization.

Critics of Marx, however, have denied this possibility and sought to show that the concept of "productive forces" is itself incoherent. Gordon Leff, for example, argues that it is impossible to conceive "of a productive force which is not also a productive relation" since organization is as "inherent" in the forces of production as tools are. He continues:

The consequences of this interpretation are far-reaching. . . . The first is that if there is no actual distinction between the forces of production and production relations the contradiction between them is not the motive force of change; if a productive relation is inherent in a productive force they are no more entities to be juxtaposed than are the heart and brain; they are each inseparable from the ensemble which they compose.[64]

According to Leff, because one finds productive forces only in a certain organization of production, the former cannot be distinguished from the latter. Leff makes an unacceptable move from the fact that productive forces, generally speaking, exist in production relations to the statement that organization is just as inherent in the productive forces as the instruments of production are. Instruments are "inherent" in the productive forces because they are a subset of the set of things that make up the productive forces: they are part of what "productive forces" denotes, while organization is "inherent" in the productive forces only in the sense that productive forces have to be arranged into relations in order that production may proceed. Leff would be constrained on his own usage to say that the human heart is "inherent" in the brain, and vice versa, which is intuitively quite odd.

Leff desires not only that the productive forces be "meaningfully distinguished" from production relations but also that each category be able to stand alone in a "tangible way."[65] One is hard pressed to imagine what kind of things would satisfy his injunction. Hearts and brains may not exist apart from one another, but they are distinguishable and can be studied independently. Further, these two organs can be juxtaposed in the sense that the motion of one may conflict with the requirements of the other (a coronary attack "contradicts" the brain's need for oxygen).

There seems no ground, then, for contending that the concept "productive forces" is conceptually muddled or incoherent. It is important to remember that Marx's definition is technical and does not rely on one's intuitions alone about what is properly "productive" or a "force." Once the elements have been identified which compose the "productive forces," it is no argument against Marx that they usually appear in "relations" or that they are connected to things which are not productive forces. The nature of the relations which link the productive forces together in the production process is the subject of the rest of this chapter.

Relations of Production

So far I have been discussing "productive forces" and have tried to present a clearer picture of this concept than is usually found in the literature on Marx. I have argued that the productive forces are best understood as being constituted by the elements—means of production and labor-power—of production. The "relations of production" with which I shall now be concerned are those relations within which production is carried on. Although such relations are of different kinds, productive forces—along with persons—are the terms which are joined by all relations of production, and it is this which provides a degree of conceptual economy to Marx's theory of historical change.

Two Types of Relations

The process of production always and necessarily involves men in some relations with each other and the means of production. To produce any given use-value, the forces of production must be in certain definite relations. The actual relations within which production proceeds are designated here as the "work" relations of production: that is, the material, technical relations which govern the actual labor process itself, abstracted from its socially and historically specific form. Obviously, though, the nature of production requires relations other than work relations: "In order to produce, [men] enter into definite connections and relations with one another and only within these social connections and relations does their action on nature, does production, take place."[66] These relations include not only the actual manner in which men work on nature but also the relations within which they regulate their mutual access to the productive forces and, as a consequence, to the products of production. Since these latter relations, generally speaking, have to do with property or ownership, I designate them "ownership" relations of production. Relations of production, whether "ownership" or "work," are not episodes or particular transactions but "relatively enduring relations" within which such episodes occur.[67] The work relations in a factory do not alter or lapse when the producers sleep at night. This is even easier to see with "ownership" relations: a man does not cease to own something when he is engaged in an activity which does not implicate that ownership. The aggregate of these relations—in which the agents of production stand with respect to nature and one another and in which they produce—forms the economic structure of society.[68]

Marx's concept Produktionsverhältnisse covers both types of relations, but I do not argue that Marx himself explicitly distinguished the two. I nurture this distinction, only implicit in his writings, in order to sharpen the analysis of "relations of production" and to introduce greater clarity into the discussion of Marx. Although it would seem surprising that Marx did not use "relations of production" to refer to work relations (after all, the word itself would seem to dictate it), this is maintained by the writers discussed in the last section (pp. 25–27), as well as by John Plamenatz.[69]

The rationale for such a view is drawn from the "Preface" where Marx writes:

At a certain stage of development, the material productive forces of society come into conflict with the existing relations of production or—what is but a legal expression for the same thing—with the property relations within the framework of which they have operated hitherto. From forms of development of the productive forces these relations turn into their fetters.

Plamenatz demarks two types of relations, similar to those which I have designated as "work" and "ownership" relations of production, which he considers as candidates for the title "relations of production." He maintains that only relations of the second type (ownership) satisfy the requirements, which the "Preface" stipulates, of (1) being capable of turning from "forms of development" of the productive forces into their "fetters," and (2) being capable of legal expression; consequently, only they are "relations of production." In the above passage Marx probably has ownership relations of production in mind, but this does not suffice to excise work relations from the "relations of production." Even if there were a reason why Marx should be taken as specifying the characteristics of *all* types of relations of production, it is uncertain that only ownership relations comply with the "Preface." Work relations could fulfill Plamenatz's first requirement: they may "fetter" or be "forms of development" of the productive forces. Further, not all instances of ownership relations meet this requirement, that is, actually turn into "fetters" of specific productive forces; does Plamenatz want to hold, in response to this, that only ownership relations are potentially able to do so? As to the second requirement, work relations often enjoy legal expression: for example, the relations of apprenticeship or of a foreman to his crew (regarding, say, the former's authority, the length and type of work, or the number of breaks).

In addition more positive textual evidence may be cited against Plamenatz. For instance, in the *Communist Manifesto*, Marx and Engels' rather eulogistic obituary of the bougeoisie, the following is written: "The bourgeoisie cannot exist without constantly revolutionizing the instruments of production, and thereby the relations of production, and with them the whole relations of society."[70] If "relations of production" is read as "ownership" relations only, then the passage is made, if not senseless, at least odd: because while the bourgeoisie perform the historical task of destroying feudal property, they are not continually revolutionizing their own order of ownership relations. The bourgeoisie expand this order and attempt to remake the world in their own image, but they accomplish this, essentially, by their willingness to introduce new productive forces and to modify and develop continually the work relations which embrace those forces. These are the relations of production which they are "constantly revolutionizing." As the second volume of *Capital* puts it:

Only the capitalist production of commodities has become an epoch-making mode of exploitation, which, in the course of its historical development, revolutionizes, through the organization of the labor-process and the enormous improvement of technique, the entire economic structure of society in a manner eclipsing all former epochs.[71]

That Marx had work relations of production within his purview in this passage from the *Manifesto* is shown by the fact that it is quoted without comment as a footnote to a paragraph in *Capi-*

tal where Marx is clearly talking about the character of such technical relations under capitalism.[72] Elsewhere, in discussing the flexible nature of labor under capitalism, he compares this with the traditional nature of slave labor, whose relations of production do not vary.[73] Here, "relations of production" indicates work relations since the labor process in slavery, Marx thought, follows only a traditional pattern.

Both kinds of relations—work and ownership—are properly subsumed under the rubric "relations of production." These two subspecies of relations, although distinguishable, are often represented by the same behavior. Since, broadly speaking, "work" relations designate the technical, material, or natural side of production while "ownership" relations mark its socially determined character, an analogy would be the contrast between sexual intercourse (a "material" relation), on the one hand, and the social relationships, such as fornication, adultery, or monogamy, in which it occurs, on the other. In any type of society, the forces of production must be united, or brought into certain relations, but these connections involve not just work relations but, simultaneously, ownership relations of production. When *The Poverty of Philosophy* says that "the modern workshop, which depends on the application of machinery, is a social production relation," both types of production relations are embraced.[74]

Although the two types of production relations—work and ownership—are intimately connected (and, indeed, the former occur only within the framework of the latter), the distinction between them is central to Marx's thought. Failure to distinguish society's technical (material) work relations from its socially specific ownership relations—that is, from the socio-historical integument of those work relations—leads to mystification, especially in the analysis of capitalism. Thus, Marx pointedly criticizes those who confuse "the material production relations with their historical and social determination."[75]

A word needs to be mentioned here about the concept "mode of production." Although arguably the key notion within historical materialism,[76] nowhere is it formulated with precision. Marx occasionally uses Produktionsweise in the restricted sense of the technical nature or manner of producing: "The production of surplus value . . . is the specific end and aim . . . of capitalist production, quite apart from any changes in the *mode of production*, which may arise from the subordination of labor to capital."[77] In the same vein, Marx speaks of "constant daily revolutions in the *mode of production*."[78] Marxist literature, however, has traditionally employed "mode of production" in the second meaning which Marx gives it, namely, that of the *social* system (or manner or mode) of production. Consider, for example, the first sentence of the first chapter of *Capital*: "The wealth of those societies, in which the capitalist *mode of production* prevails, presents itself as 'an immense accumulation of commodities.'"[79]

In this sense, the term denotes the kind of production which is carried on within a certain set of ownership production relations. Marx uses "mode of production," in a fashion which is more encompassing than "economic structure," to refer to the manner of producing which takes place both within and as a result of the given ownership relations of production. Thus, capitalist relations of production define a certain kind of connection between men and the productive forces; the capitalist mode of production, on the other hand, involves the production of commodities, a certain manner of obtaining surplus, labor-time determination of value, a tendency to expand the productive forces, and so on. A "mode of production" is intended by Marx to signify, rather generally, a system of producing, a distinct and independent way of carrying on social production as this is determined by an economic structure characterized by a specific ownership relation of production.

Work Relations

In any production process a variety of intertwined work relations will be required. Work relations structure the labor process, but they are not that process. Because work relations are generally viewed with regard to the production of specific use-values (rather than, say, the production of exchange-value), it is the individual character of the relation(s) which is relevant, since this determines whether the items being produced are horse-shoes or automobiles. A question, however, arises: Are men in such nonindustrial jobs as banking, retail sales, or entertainment to be considered in "work" relations of production?

In this regard, the "Preface" must be consulted, and Marx makes it clear that he is concerned with the "mode of production of *material* life": "In the social production of their existence, men enter into definite . . . relations of production which correspond to a definite stage of development of their *material* productive forces [my emphasis]." Marx is not referring here to what he elsewhere calls the materialized or objectified productive forces (the means of production) but rather to the (productive) forces of material production. It has been implicit in the discussion heretofore of "productive forces" and "relations of production" that "material" production is what is at issue, but what is material production? The answer is simply that material production is the production of material things.*

Work relations are those involved in the production of mate-rial objects, relations which comprise the actual production process viewed apart from its social framework. Owing to the historical form of that production, a whole range of other relations—such as banking and retail sales—may be required for that production to continue, but these relations should not be identified as part of the "work" relations of production. Since work relations concern the material reproduction of society as a whole, they do not exist in isolation from one another. The more developed production is, the more complicated is the intercon-nection of work relations; the work relations in any factory are conditioned by their connection with a whole network of com-plementary relations.

Since work relations link labor-power with the means of pro-duction, this might suggest that work relations are in fact rela-

*Theories of Surplus Value 1: 285–87. Rival answers to this question might be that material production is the production of (a) use-values, (b) commodities, (c) surplus-value, or (d) those things necessary for material life. None of these candidates are theoretically satisfactory.

tions between productive forces, rather than between persons and other persons or productive forces. A weaker claim might be that at least some work relations need not engage persons. ("Ownership" relations surely seem to implicate persons, since productive forces cannot own each other; so the question is whether "work" relations are analogous.) In regard to the first suggestion, it is correct to observe that what is required in a particular work relation is labor-power of a certain type and not individual A or B. Nonetheless, labor-power is only borne by persons, so that any relation involving labor-power must also involve at least one person.

The reason that this consequence is not unhappy is also the motive for scotching the second claim: relations of production are *social* relations, relations involving men. Instruments could hardly form a *social* relation of production. The means of production, naturally, may demand specific relations if they are to operate efficiently, or at all, but even under the most advanced technology (imagine a completely computerized factory) the means of production would be under the control of some human agency. They would not constitute a relation of production themselves because it is only in terms of man that production is defined.

Relations of production must incorporate at least one human agent. But is the *social* requirement satisfied with only one such agent? When an individual owns a productive force, there is a sense in which this is a social relation (even though it may involve no other individual) because the notion of ownership is defined only with reference to other men—that is, in a social context. Marx supports this, as well as its obverse: namely, that it makes no sense to speak of an isolated individual with property.[80] Work relations of production in such a case are, arguably, on a par with ownership relations. An isolated man produces and has relations with tools, but this is not social production; it is survival. Relations of production—whether work or ownership—is a concept which is just not applicable to such a situation. What this suggests, turning to the case of one individual in a work relation to a productive force or forces but this time *in* society, is that this is a relation of production because it takes place within a social context.[81]

To resume the examination of these work relations, it is clear that, in general, they respond to the nature of the productive forces. This is true particularly for the instruments of production: "Labor is organized, is divided differently according to the instruments it disposes over. The hand-mill presupposes a different division of labor from the steam-mill. Thus it is slapping history in the face to want to begin by the division of labor in general."[82] But this should not be understood as a tautology. Nor should the determination of the work relations be seen simply as the consequence of the influence of the means of production alone rather than of that other part of the productive forces as well, labor-power. H. B. Acton appears to make both mistakes: "Marx is quite right in saying that means of production determine the organization of labor. . . . Different types of tool or machine determine different types of job-relations."[83]

First, it is not just the means of production which determine the nature of the work relations; rather, the work relations are largely dependent upon the skill and experience of the labor-power engaged. At a low level of technology with simple tools, work relations will hinge greatly on the proficiency of labor-power in employing the means of production in the most efficient way. But even at a higher level of production, it is not enough to have just certain means of production, Marx tells us. Workmen with the appropriate expertise are also required for production to be possible: "The expansion of industries carried on by means of machinery, and the invasion by machinery of fresh branches of production, were dependent on the growth of a class of workmen, who, owing to the almost artistic nature of their employment, could increase their numbers only gradually, and not by leaps and bounds."[84]

Secondly, the fact that work relations of production connect productive forces should not be taken to mean that it is a tautology to say that the productive forces determine the work relations. Acton, as I have suggested, appears to hold that it is a tautology, and indeed elsewhere he affirms his belief that "technology invention can *necessitate* changes in job-relations but only *favor* changes" in ownership relations of production.[85] There is good reason for Marx, however, why the set of society's available productive forces does not logically necessitate its work relations: it is, simply, that a discrepancy between the productive forces and the relations of production is possible. In a crisis, for example, when the productive forces lie idle, there is an obvious disparity between them and the work relations which should be occupying them in production. Indeed, it is perfectly appropriate within Marx's framework to speak of work relations being more or less efficient, productive, or compatible with regard to a set of productive forces. This does not imply that Marx holds that the productive forces do not determine work relations; on the contrary, it is just because the productive forces do not logically necessitate work relations—because they can be in better or worse relations—that Marx can hold, as he does, that the productive forces tend to bring about the work relations appropriate to their optimal exploitation.

New or improved productive forces may require different work relations if they are to be properly yoked for production. Whether such relations come about is to a large extent determined by the nature of that other type of relations of production, namely, ownership relations, which I now examine.

Ownership Relations

It should already be apparent that the nature of the ownership relations may shape in certain ways the work relations, which relations provide the former's content. Capitalist relations, for example, facilitate the development of, among other things, cooperative and socialized work relations. Slave ownership relations of production, by contrast, generally encourage labor-intensive work relations or, at any rate, restrict the means of production to a crude level.[86] Ownership relations of production are the relations which regulate control over and access to the productive forces in the material process of production. They encompass relations of ownership of the productive forces as well as those relations which involve such ownership: for example, that a man hires out his labor-power implies that he owns it. In addition, certain kindred ownership-type relations may be identified.

At least three broad kinds of these latter relations can be discerned. First are those relations which, although they are not relations of immediate material production, may be necessitated in different ways by the socially specific manner in which production is carried on. For example, the circulation and marketing of commodities under capitalism is not material production for Marx, even though such spheres greatly heighten the efficiency of capitalist production. Banking is similarly contingent on the type of ownership relations of production and the nature of production within those relations. The agents occupied in these activities do stand in certain relations of ownership to particular productive forces—the merchant or banker has capital, which could be converted into means of production, and his workers have their labor-power—but these are not relations in which material production directly ensues. This leads to a second type of relation: relations which, although they depend in a fashion upon the ownership relations of production, are not required by the nature of production under those relations—for example, a domestic servant employed by a capitalist to wait on him. Here the servant is able to lease his labor-power and the capitalist is in a position to hire it because of their respective relations to the productive forces, despite the fact that the servant-capitalist relation does not involve them in material production.

The capitalist is not engaged in a capitalistic relation with his valet because the servant does not produce surplus value for his employer. Capitalist relations can, however, occur outside of material production, as Marx makes clear in *Capital*: for example, when an entrepreneur invests "in a teaching factory, instead of a sausage factory."[87] This contrasts with the first type of relations above, relations which are not—according to Marx—directly productive of surplus value, and presents a third kind of ownership-like relation, one which seems to have no analogue in other economic formations.

Although Marx does not specifically address the issue, I think these three relations should not be reckoned among the "relations of production." The fact that one has any sort of connection with the productive forces is not enough to situate him within society's Produktionsverhältnisse since these are man's relations within material production. The relations examined above reflect but are not part of the relations of production. Thus, in my view, the economic structure—the totality of the relations of production, both work and ownership—does not encompass everything one might think of as economic in a broad sense, but it does incorporate Marx's four spheres of material production (manufacture, mining, agriculture, and transportation), and this would seem enough to do justice to the title "economic." If, however, a workable criterion were advanced which included the relations which I have been discussing (or some of them) within the "relations of production," the course of my subsequent discussion will not be undermined because these relations are still either dependent on, or of secondary importance to, "ownership" relations of production in the narrow sense.

It is characteristic of a social formation to subsume under its dominant type of ownership relations other relations which have nothing to do with material production. All the spheres of bourgeois social life, for example, reflect commodity relations, and those of feudalism personal dependence. A man becomes a slave because of his specific relations to society's productive forces and because of the nature of that society's production relations. If, however, he tutors his master's children in Greek instead of working in the fields, then he is not in a relation of material production. His social existence, of course, is determined by that society's production relations. Now this slave would no doubt be numbered among the slave class by Marxian analysis, but—as I shall suggest in a later section—this is because of his resemblance to the authentic members of that class of slaves, which is formed by the material relations of production; his class connection, in this case, cannot be used to situate him within a relation of production. If wealthy Britons could legally own Africans so long as they did not employ them in material production, this group of blacks, strictly speaking, would not constitute an economic class as Marx understands it.

Some sociologists, concerned with elaborating a theory of classes, have found Marx's conception of production relations an inadequate theoretical basis, but their interpretation of "relations of production" fails to do justice to Marx. Ralf Dahrendorf, for example, asks: "Does Marx understand, by the relations of property or production, the relations of factual control and subordination in the enterprises of industrial production—or merely the authority relations insofar as they are based on the legal title of property?" This is how he answers his question: "It can be shown that [Marx's] analysis is based on the narrow, legal concept of property."[88] Dahrendorf does not actually bother to *show* this, and this is not surprising since Marx's analysis of production relations (and, thus, class relations) does not rest on a formal, juridical conception of property.

Note, though, that the problem itself is stated poorly by Dahrendorf. First, the relations of production are not just relations in the enterprises of industrial production, be they those of factual control or of authority rooted in legal property. The concept is broader. The essence of capital as an ownership relation of production rests on a specific connection of men to the productive forces, which enables the purchase of labor-power as a commodity (and thus the creation of surplus value for the capitalist). In this sense it is a relation outside and prior to the immediate production process even though this is where the relation manifests itself (it appears in men working together in production). Secondly, control and subordination in the capitalist enterprise are not, for Marx, simply of one kind. He discriminates between control which is necessitated by the very nature of the labor process (for example, large-scale cooperation which requires supervision) and control which is due to the peculiar nature of the ownership relations of production and displays the antagonism between the capitalist and the wage-laborer.

An examination of feudal ownership relations as Marx conceives them, furthermore, demonstrates that his theory involves a more sophisticated conception of Produktionsverhältnisse than Dahrendorf allows. In feudalism the direct producer is not the owner but merely the possessor of both his means of production and his labor-power because his surplus labour, or at least a good portion of it, belongs to the landlord.[89] In contradiction to the modern concept of property, it is important to realize that in the case of feudal relations, ownership of, say, the instruments of production was not entirely the prerogative of either the feudal lord or the serf. The serf had possession of them, but the lord had an entitlement to a portion of the serf's product. Despite his power, the lord generally speaking could not deprive the serf of these instruments—his title to them, as modern jurists say, was not "clear"; rather, it was bound up with reciprocal obligations.[90]

To take a different case, Marx and Engels frequently describe the modern peasant as only a "phantom" or "nominal" owner of his means of production. The peasant's property ceases to provide him with independence since by means of credit, mortgages, and taxation, the usurers, lawyers, banks, and state gain control over it. Simple peasant proprietorship, a historically doomed survival of a past mode of production, is transmogrified by its subjection to the dominant capitalist mode of production. "Peasant proprietorship itself has become nominal, leaving to the peasant the delusion of proprietorship, and expropriating him from the fruits of his own labor."[91] Leaving aside mortgages (insofar as they dilute the peasant's legal title), the peasant, then, no longer enjoys "real" ownership since he is deprived—because of his weak and exploited economic position—of the de facto fruits of his property. In Marx's view, production relations in the country had altered such that, while the peasant still possessed the agricultural productive forces, he no longer retained effective economic control over them or their products.

The ownership relations of production are actually the relations of control over the productive forces and their products, relations of control which are not necessarily identifiable with "ownership" or "property" in a modern sense. Slavery, feudalism, and capitalism each entail a different kind of ownership relation of production (both in the things owned and in the way in which they can be "owned")—a distinct relation between men in the appropriation of the productive forces and products of production. For this reason, a limited legalistic view of "relations of production" cannot, pace Dahrendorf, be ascribed to Marx.

It may also be observed that Marx frequently wielded legal terms in nonlegal senses. Thus, Marx refers to means of production which were "in fact, or legally, the property of the tiller himself," and, somewhat later in the same text, he discusses means of production becoming the tiller's property, first in fact and then also "legally."[92] In the same vein, the first volume of *Capital* mentions private peasant property being hidden under feudal title.[93] Such examples betoken a usage which is *not* "based on the narrow, legal concept of property."

Marx's requirement, in fact, for discriminating between economic formations is far from simple legal ownership: "The essential difference between the various economic forms of society, between, for instance, a society based on slave-labor, and one based on wage-labor, lies only in the mode in which this surplus-labor is in each case extracted from the actual producer, the laborer."[94] The specific manner in which unpaid labor is wrung out of the immediate producers "determines the relationship of rulers and ruled, as it grows directly out of production."[95] The connection of the rulers to the direct producers, as this emanates from their respective relations to the productive forces, defines the specific character of the mode of production, and one important aspect of Marxian analysis is to demonstrate how given ownership relations determine a particular method of pumping a surplus out of the laborers. Because this extraction is the essence of any mode of production, Marx perceives the distribution relations of society as springing from the specific social form of the production process and of the relations between men: "The specific distribution relations are thus merely the expression of the specific historical production relations."* Thus, every kind of property or ownership brings with it a distinctive way of extracting a surplus and allotting the products of labor.

In this light, capitalist (ownership) production relations can be seen to involve more than the respective connections of capitalist and laborer to the productive forces: they also import a specific mode of siphoning off a surplus. Capitalist ownership relations are relations which allow for and oversee the expropriation of unpaid labor from the working class, an extraction which requires that the two classes have different, specific ties to the productive forces. Ownership relations then are not only relations of ownership (in whatever historical meaning) among men, but are simultaneously relations which structure society's allocation of the products of labor and govern the general motion of the mode of production.

Property

A central tenet of Marx's materialist conception is that what is understood as "property" in any society is in fact the result, or "expression," of the actual social relations of production—what

---

*Capital 3: 882 (*Werke* 25: 889). Methodologically, this is significant for Marx's approach, since it explains why one cannot begin with economic categories, like profit, simply as they present themselves every day: "The wage presupposes wage-labor, and profit—capital. These definite forms of distribution thus presuppose definite social characteristics of production conditions, and definite social relations of production agents." See also *Grundrisse* (Penguin ed.), p. 758 (Dietz ed., p. 644). At *Grundrisse*, pp. 88–100 (Dietz ed., pp. 10–20), Marx attempts a more abstract defense of the ascendancy of production over distribution.

I have designated the "ownership relations of production." "Property" here means property relations in a juridical sense.

In each historical epoch, property has developed differently and under a set of entirely different social relations. Thus to define bourgeois property is nothing else than to give an exposition of all the social relations of bourgeois production.[96]

The property of a different epoch, feudal property, develops in a series of entirely different social relations.[97]

Man's relations of production do not come about because a given type of property exists; rather, the kind of property occurs because of certain social relations.

It has been observed elsewhere that Marx intended a "naming" relation in the "Preface" between legal terms and (ownership) relations of production.[98] This is clear from the passages just quoted as well as from Marx's reference to the "social relations forming in their entirety *what is* today *known* as property."[99] Marx also held that property relations are the effects of the relations of production; that is to say, the relations of production give rise to specific types of legal relations.[100]

The relevant type of Produktionsverhältnisse in this context is what I have called the "ownership" relations, but they should be understood in a nonlegal, nonnormative sense as the relations of control over the productive forces. In simple commodity production, for example, each individual producer owns the requisite means of production for the performance of his labor; by virtue of this the product of his labor is his possession. This grounds the exchange of his product for that of another independent producer. The two producers, Marx says,

must, therefore, mutually recognize each other as private proprietors. This juridical relation, whose form is the contract, whether now legally developed or not, is a relation between two wills, in which the economic relation is reflected. The content of this juridical or will relation is given by the economic relation itself.[101]

The economic relation here consists of the producers' respective relations of control over certain productive forces and products.

On this basis a reciprocal acknowledgment of rights—a juristic relation entered into by two "wills"—is possible, and this permits exchange.

The economic relation is different in capitalism, where the laborers are forced (by necessity) to sell their labor-power to the owners of the means of production, who are consequently able to appropriate the product of the workers' labor. This is the essence of capitalist property. Formally and legally, it manifests in a juridical relation between an independent buyer and an independent seller of labor-power and in the legal entitlement of the capitalist to the entire product which he employs the labor-power in producing. I shall have more to say about this later, but here it should be stressed that for Marx the legal relations—that is, the property relations—rest on more primary "ownership" relations; these "ownership" relations pertain to the types of control or power over the productive forces which characterize the capitalist and the laborer, respectively.

Because of this, Marx concentrates on the nature of the "ownership" relations of production: "To try to give a definition of property as of [sic] an independent relation, a category apart, an abstract and eternal idea, can be nothing but an illusion of metaphysics or jurisprudence."[102] For Marx, such an illusory outlook marks the ideological approach: namely, dealing with legal effects as if they were independent, or even determining, of relations of production. Marx and Engels' *camera obscura* metaphor suggests that this illusion—more like a mirage than a hallucination—has an objective basis, and they acknowledge that property relations in the legal sense may become somewhat divorced from the production relations which they represent: this happens in the modern state when through the division of labor a judiciary arises with an interest in making legal relations internally coherent.[103]

It is not clear whether the fact that legal relations are able to grain some independence from the relations of production is, for Marx, the cause or the effect of the "juridical illusion" that they are completely independent of them. Nonetheless, the functional necessity of legalized relations is not lessened by their becoming codified and the subject of purely legalistic reasoning:

It is in the interest of the ruling section of society to sanction the existing order as law and to legally establish its limits given through usage and tradition. . . . And such regulation and order are themselves indispensible elements of any mode of production, if it is to assume social stability and independence from mere chance and arbitrariness.[104]

Because the legal system represents and legitimates the given organization of economic relations generally and in an abstract fashion, the immediate interests of a particular member of the ruling class may run counter to it—but not, according to the theory, the long-run welfare of the class as a whole.

Legal relations, thus, provide social stability. In addition, the transactions which take place on the basis of a certain kind of property often conceal the actual production relations in which that property is rooted. As examples, Marx offers the buying and selling of land or Negroes:

But the title itself is simply transferred, and not created by the sale. The title must exist before it can be sold, and a series of sales can no more create this title through continued repetition than a single sale can. What created it in the first place were the production relations.[105]

Land or Negroes only become "property," the subject matter of certain legal relations, within the context of definite relations of production. The juristic forms in which economic transactions appear do not determine their content; they merely express it.

But the fact, as Marx observes in the *Grundrisse*, that man realizes production not through his relationships as expressed in thought but through his active, real relationships implies that these former relations are amenable to change.[106] Accordingly, the above passage continues:

As soon as these [production relations] have reached a point where they must shed their skin [*umhäuten*], the material source of the title, justified economically and historically and arising from the process which creates social life, falls by the wayside, along with all transactions based upon it.

Closely related to this is Marx's belief that the justice of the particular transactions between agents of production depends on whether they occur as a natural consequence of the production relations—not on their content. "This content is just whenever it corresponds, is appropriate, to the mode of production. It is unjust whenever it contradicts that mode."[107]

The fact that transactions concerning property and ownership may actually conceal the relations which make them possible is particularly significant in the relation between wage-labor and capital. As mentioned above, in the purchase of labor-power, the owner of money and the owner of labor-power enter into the relation of buyer and seller, a money relation. Their class relationship, however, is presupposed from the moment the two face each other, and this relationship occurs because the means of production and subsistence are separated from the owner of labor-power, being the property of another.[108] Accordingly Marx emphasizes that it is necessary to study relations as a whole, "not in their *legal* expression as *voluntary relations* but in their real form, that is, as *relations of production.*"[109] In the case of capitalism it is exactly this juridically voluntary relation between the laborer and the capitalist that obscures two crucial facts: (1) that the laborer has no real choice but to sell his labor-power, and (2) that this sale of his labor-power only reproduces his need to continue selling it. The reason for this abstruseness is precisely that although the laborer is free vis à vis any particular capitalist, he is in bondage to the capitalist class as a whole.

In feudalism, on the other hand, as in slavery, the actual relations of production are concealed within relations of personal domination and servitude between men, relations "which appear and are evident as the direct motive power of the process of production."* (Here, as elsewhere in Marx, "appearance" contrasts with "essence.") Ownership relations support the traditional, customary (in a sense, legalistic) relation of lord and serf. The gist of feudal production is that the lord is in a position

---

Capital 3: 831 (*Werke* 25: 839). Only under capitalism, writes Marx, is the exploitation relation separated "from all patriarchal and political or also religious entanglements [Verquickungen]." "Resultate des Unmittelbaren Produktionprozesses," p. 102 (ms. p. 473).

to appropriate gratuitously a portion of the serf's labor, but this naked exploitation (this "tangibly open secret") is, in fact, obscured by the vassalage relation in which it appears, just as in bourgeois society legalistic relations conceal the actual nature of the "ownership" relations involved.*

Both customary feudal relations and bourgeois legal relations perform the necessary function of stabilizing the economic structure by expressing and codifying that reality; on the other hand, they tend to mask the real nature of the relations of production. In capitalism the "fictio juris of a contract" between free agents ensures the imperceptibility of those "invisible threads" which bind the wage-laborer to capital.[110] In feudalism the true character of the social relations of production is hidden by the relations of personal dependence which also characterize the other spheres of feudal life.[111] This is something, however, which can only be detected by examining the relations, not between individuals, but between whole classes. Here, a few words are required about the linking of classes to production relations, since this is a cardinal component of Marxian analysis.

Classes

Instead of a systematic exposition of this issue, Marx left only a formal introduction; the last chapter of *Capital*, entitled "Classes," breaks off after only a few lines. Yet the core of his view is limpid. For Engels and Marx, all ownership relations of production in recorded history have been class relations—that is, a certain class of people in society has been privileged in regard to the productive forces. (This, however, did not mean that production had always involved class relations, or that it need always dictate them; Marx and Engels believed that primitive man had produced communally and, of course, that socialism would again reestablish classless production relations.) Persons

---

*Under feudalism, it is evident that a surplus product is extracted, but the utilitarian character of the production relations is concealed; the situation is reversed under capitalism. See G. A. Cohen, "Karl Marx and the Withering Away of Social Science," pp. 190–91.

or groups of persons standing in a similar ownership relation of production form a definable class.

Economically demarcated classes are also classes in a social sense essentially because members of the same class tend to view the world in a similar way. Marx embroiders this in his discussion of the Legitimists and Orleanists in *The Eighteenth Brumaire of Louis Bonaparte*:

> What kept the two factions apart, therefore, was not any so-called principles, it was their material conditions of existence, two different kinds of property, it was the old contrast between town and country, the rivalry between capital and landed property. . . . Upon the different forms of property, upon the social conditions of existence, rises an entire superstructure of distinct and peculiarly formed sentiments, illusions, modes of thought and views of life. The entire class creates and forms them out of its material foundations and out of the correponding social relations.[112]

The ideology of the ruling class, on the other hand, does tend to predominate over that of the other classes because of the ruling class's hegemony over intellectual as well as material production; the class which has the means of material production at its disposal usually controls the means of mental production.[113] Marx goes on in the above passage to mention the relation of the individual to the ideology of his class, but what is relevant here is his view that the opinions and behavior of classes grow out of the relations of production. He refers, for example, to "the movement of the working-class on both sides of the Atlantic, which grew instinctively out of the relations of production themselves."[114] Classes and their representatives are treated in *Capital* only insofar as they are the bearers of certain economic relations,[115] but in general the conduct of both capitalists and laborers issues from and reflects the relations in which they have been situated.[116]

That some particular classes but not others spring up is a consequence of the nature of production in a given period, but the basic historical explanation for class rule itself, as Engels explains it, is the transformation of a social division of labor into a relation of oppression and exploitation. As soon as it is no longer materially mandatory for everyone to work in order to sustain society—as soon as it becomes possible for some members of society to live off the labor of others—classes arise. The ruling class rationalizes its domination by the need to control and govern production as well as to "look after the intellectual work of society."[117] Since the beginning of civilization, production has proceeded within the antogonism between different orders, estates, and classes, and it is only this which has allowed the development of the productive forces by forcing the productivity of the direct producers above the subsistence level. "No antagonism, no progress."[118] Such a historical apology crumbles when production has reached the level of proficiency which characterizes modern capitalism.

If classes for Marx are defined with regard to their roles in production—that is, by the relations of production—it is precisely because Marx approaches production from the vantage point of classes that he feels he is able to reveal pellucidly the nature of production, essentially by displaying how the process of production continually reproduces the relations of production.[119] As Marx says: "The matter takes quite another aspect, when we contemplate, not the single capitalist, and the single laborer, but the capitalist class and the laboring class, not an isolated process of production, but capitalist production in full swing, and on its actual social scale."[120] A few comments, however, have to be made about the connection of this economic account of classes to their social reality.

First, it needs stressing that in his analysis of capitalism Marx employs a very abstract model, and this is why he is primarily concerned with two classes, workers and capitalists. He does not suppose that this does justice to the actual class structure in capitalism ("which by no means consists only of two classes, workers and industrial capitalists") but rather that it permits him to explicate the essence of that mode of production.[121] Thus, there is a scientific reason for the two class schema in *Capital*, a justification which is strengthened by Marx's belief that it also reflects the direction of capitalist evolution.[122]

Secondly, Marx occasionally distinguishes between a class for-itself and a class in-itself. The *Manifesto of the Communist Party* describes the various stages of development of the proletariat until "the collisions between individual workmen and individual bourgeois take more and more the character of collisions between two classes."[123] This movement is succinctly reviewed in *The Poverty of Philosophy*:

Economic conditions had first transformed the mass of the people of the country into workers. The combination of capital has created for this mass a common situation, common interests. This mass is thus already a class as against capital, but not yet for itself. In the struggle, of which we have noted only a few phases, this mass becomes united, and constitutes itself as a class for itself. The interests it defends become class interests. But the struggle of class against class is a political struggle.[124]

In Marx's early works such a distinction is given a rather philosophical (if not idealistic) underpinning,[125] but it is a contrast which is latent in *The Eighteenth Brumaire*'s famous discussion of the French peasantry[126] and in the mature Marx's emphasis on the importance of the proletariat organizing itself politically as a class.[127]

Thirdly, when Marx talks more concretely about classes in a particular society, he often seems to utilize a rougher gauge than the economic criterion of "relations of production." For example, it was said earlier that a domestic servant was not in a relation of production, but I think that Marx and subsequent Marxists would not hesitate to locate such a person within the working class because he—just like an industrial worker—owns nothing but his labor-power. Similarly, the bourgeois class gets expanded to encompass not just capitalists but also their wealthy non-owning lackeys (like politicians), their wives and their offspring. This is because classes, while they may be designated by their members' occupancy of similar relations of production, also enjoy identifiable social traits and a common world-view; thus, individuals sharing the latter lineaments but not all the requisites of that class's relations of production tend to be counted within that class; for example, retired workers or the non-working children of workers are called "working class." This nonetheless is a small and basically terminological issue compared to the problem facing contemporary adherents of Marxist economics, which is to justify Marx's abstractions in the light of a very much more complex economic reality; or to the problem facing his modern political partisans in the West, which is to ascertain the class (and, hence, political allegiance) of such large twentieth-century occupational groups as white-collar workers, semi-professionals, and skilled technicians.

Nicos Poulantzas, contrary to what I have been saying, believes it is a mistake (namely, "economism") to define social classes by the relations of production—that is (in his words), to reduce social classes to the economic alone. His objection is not that the reality of a class involves much more than its particular relations of production (which is what was discussed above), but rather that the concept itself refers to *"the ensemble of the structures* of a mode of production and social formation, *and to the relations which are maintained there* by the different levels."[128] Or put less technically, "social classes are defined not simply by their relation to the economic, but also by their relation to the political and ideological levels."[129] This does not mean that a plurality of criteria define a social class, but that a class has "one perfectly defined criterion, which is a complex relation to the level of structures, levels which are themselves perfectly defined."*

What Poulantzas would appear to have in mind is that the mode of production determines all the various spheres or structures of society (economic, ideological, etc.) coincidentally, so that as a result a class is emplaced simultaneously in certain positions in all those structures. Although I shall spare the reader a further account of Poulantzas, it should be clear that his interpretation is at odds with Marx's opinion that classes have their

*Nicos Poulantzas, *Political Power and Social Classes*, p. 70n. The phrase "perfectly defined" is a small monument to the ability of some French Marxists to solve thorny theoretical issues by refusing to acknowledge their existence.

particular ideas, beliefs, and political commitments because of the economic position which they inhabit. To ascribe a class's characteristics to it *by definition*—which is approximately what Poulantzas does—would seem to remove most of the explanatory interest (and most of the materialist content) from Marx's position.

CHAPTER TWO

Marx's Technological Determinism

> Technology discloses man's mode of dealing with
> Nature, the process of production by which he
> sustains his life, and thereby also lays bare the
> mode of formation of his social relations, and of
> the mental conceptions that flow from them.
>
> —*Capital* 1: 372n

So FAR I have been explicating two of the basic concepts of
Marx's theory of history. Since relatively little attention has
been paid to unraveling these important notions, the exercise of
the first chapter may have some value in its own right, if only in
offering a fresh perspective on a variety of issues in Marx's
thought. For the specific purposes of the present study, however, it was required that these key concepts of historical materialism be carefully unpacked. Clarification of them is necessary
for an accurate presentation of the theory and also shows that
Marx's perspective is, at least, conceptually coherent.

Now it is time to turn to the connection between the productive forces and the relations of production, as envisioned by
Marx, both within the mode of production and, more germane
to my theme, within the transition between different modes of
production. This chapter maintains that Marx perceived the
productive forces as the determining factor in historical development, and it endeavors to explicate what Marx had in
mind. Faulty conceptions of this position (often triggered by a
misconstruction of the basic terminology of historical materialism) have led some to deny that Marx intended to assign the
determining role in history to the productive forces. If, however,
investigation shows that Marx's "technological determinism" is

far from the manifest absurdity it is often taken to be, then perhaps less need will be felt to rescue Marx from himself.

Specifying the nature of the historical dialectics of productive forces and relations of production is not easy. Marx himself directs little effort toward explicating the character of productive-force determinism, and his interpreters have followed his example. Marx, at least, had the excuse of investing his energies in investigating the operation of this dynamic in the concrete. Accordingly, later chapters will be dealing with the interconnection of productive forces and relations of production in the context of the specific historical transitions which Marx discusses. These particular studies should document my "technological" interpretation of Marx and help to illustrate the type of determinism involved. By contrast, the examination in this chapter will be more general and precursory. A number of issues must be aired here in preparation for my subsequent audits of Marx's annals—what the productive forces determine, in what manner, why, and so on—but the absence of any thorough review of these and related topics by Marx himself does not allow this chapter to rely on the same kind of textual exegesis to which I had recourse earlier.

Nonetheless, my intention here is to bring out the nature of Marx's theoretical commitment as fully and consistently as is possible. Unfortunately, a number of questions which one would wish to ask of such a theory are not satisfactorily answered. Frequently, there are hints of Marx's reasons for taking a particular position, and these are interrogated where they throw light on his more explicit views; at some points Marx's shortcomings must be the end of my inquiry. My purpose is not to refurbish Marx's model of history so that it can withstand contemporary criticism, even if that were within my power. Rather, the aim is to reveal the dynamic which Marx discerned within history and, as a corollary, to demonstrate that I have not ascribed to Marx a patently untenable view—one which he could not possibly have endorsed.

That Marx opined that the productive forces are the motive

and determining factor in history is, I think, certain, but (as indicated above) the nature and consequences of this determination are not widely understood. There exists a tendency even among Marxists to reject such a "technological-determinist" rendering of Marx—either because of its technological emphasis or because of its determinism. Consequently, I shall begin by publishing a few additional passages by Marx which underscore the primacy of the productive forces. After expanding on the nature of this preeminence, in following sections I shall give the reasons for it, analyze the general character of historical explanation provided by Marx, and examine the consequences of this for productive force determinism.

The Primacy of the Productive Forces

> The multitude of productive forces accessible to
> men determines the nature of society.
> —*Selected Works* 1: 31

From much of the discussion heretofore and from the "Preface" itself, it should be clear that Marx saw the key to human history in the development of man's productive forces. They are "the material basis of all social organization;" their improvement explains the advance of society.[1] Expositors of Marx who for various reasons have wished to circumvent the ascription to Marx of such a thesis have underplayed the "Preface," treating it as an anomaly. It is worth noting, then, that the "Preface" states a view to which Marx subscribed throughout his career. Even in *The Poverty of Philosophy*, an early work which Marx continued to value in later years, the "Preface" position is explicit:

The mode of production, the relations in which productive forces are developed, are anything but eternal laws, but [rather] . . . they correspond to a definite development of men and of their productive forces, and . . . a change in men's productive forces necessarily brings about a change in their relations of production.[2]

This was a further refinement of the materialist position which he and Engels had originally endeavored to hammer out in *The German Ideology*. There, for perhaps the first time, the

emergence of higher relations of production is made dependent
upon the productive forces.

> Thus all collisions in history have their origin, according to our view, in
> the contradiction between the productive forces and the form of inter-
> course.[3]

> In the place of an earlier form of intercourse, which has become a fet-
> ter, a new one is put, corresponding to the more developed productive
> forces, and hence, to the advanced mode of the self-activity of
> individuals—a form which in its turn becomes a fetter and is then re-
> placed by another.[4]

Verkehrsform ("form of intercourse") and a few related expressions were employed at this time by Marx and Engels to
label what they were later to term "relations of production."[5]
Still, the notion which runs through Marx's mature works is already present: namely, the development and transformation of
man's relations of production as the result of his developing material production, his productive forces. Three examples:

> Each specific historical form of [the labor] process further develops its
> material foundations and social forms. Whenever a certain stage of
> maturity has been reached, the specific historical form is discarded and
> makes way for a higher one . . . [because of] the contradictions and an-
> tagonisms between the distribution relations, and thus the specific his-
> torical form of their corresponding production relations, on the one
> hand, and the productive forces, the production powers and the de-
> velopment of their agencies, on the other hand.[6]

> Thus the social relations within which individuals produce, the social
> relations of production, change, are transformed, with the change and
> development of the material means of production, the productive
> forces.[7]

> The (economic) relations and consequently the social, moral, and politi-
> cal state of nations changes with the *change* in the material powers of
> production.[8]

The "Preface" motif, illustrated in these passages, concerns historical development. Despite the reciprocal influence and dialectical interplay (stressed ad nauseum in the secondary literature)
between the relations of production and the productive forces,

Marx considered the productive forces to be the long-run determinant of historical change. To begin clarifying Marx's position, it may be helpful to distinguish between two similar assertions (as Marx himself does not): (1) that changes in the relations of production are always a result of changes in the productive forces; and (2) that changes in the productive forces always result in changed relations of production. Statement (1) but not statement (2) asserts that productive force change is *necessary* for production relations change; statement (2) but not statement (1) asserts that productive force change is *sufficient* for production relations change.

Changes in the productive forces include both improvements of the existing productive forces—that is, changes inside the given productive forces of a society—and innovations in what that society possesses as productive forces. Changes in the relations of production are alterations in the nature of man's relations to the productive forces and other men, changes either in "work" or in "ownership" connections. These do not include variations in the specific persons or productive forces which are their terms; the relevant kind of change is in the nature or type of relation. Similarly, Marx is not usually concerned with alterations of particular individual relations. Consider a small manufacture which goes out of business: that the work relations of this particular enterprise no longer exist implies a variation (although obviously minor) in that specific society's economic structure, a change in its relations of production. Marx, however, is really only interested in changes in the species (be the genus "work" or "ownership") of those relations.

Claim (2) above is that changes in the productive forces bring about modified relations, but this assertion is problematic. First, changes in the forces of production may be accommodated by the existing relations: consider a carpenter using a new, slightly improved hammer in place of his old one, or a more skilled carpenter replacing a less talented one in the same job. The relations in question may be more productive, but they are the same relations. On the other hand, it should be obvious that a productive force advance can occur without an adjustment of the type of ownership relations of production.

Secondly, the modifications required to accommodate better the existing productive forces or to utilize previously unexploited forces are by no means immediately brought into effect. Marx undoubtedly held that changes in the productive forces induce permutations in the relations of production, but in a sweepingly historical fashion: as man's productive forces develop, his relations of production, his social relations, are obliged to adapt to them. What Marx envisioned was a swelling pressure on the relations of production by the productive forces prior to any significant structural metamorphosis.

Not only must this compulsion build up substantially before fundamental alterations are realized, but, in addition, the precise nature and timing of a basic mutation of the social production relations (although not, for Marx, its basic necessity) often depend on superstructural considerations. The men who effect such a change, writes Marx in the "Preface," only become conscious of the conflict between productive forces and relations of production—and then fight it out—at an ideological (legal, political, religious) level.[9] While these arenas are not simply epiphenomena of the economic relations, they acquire their efficacy in historical change—for Marx—only because of the more fundamental pressure of the productive forces.

The idea that changes in the relations of production induced by the productive forces may not be immediately brought about, and may be influenced by superstructural factors, reveals something about Marx's conception of historical evolution, but it does not undermine, literally speaking, the sufficiency of such innovation for effecting relational alterations. In regard to the first point (that relations need not always alter in order to accommodate productive-force advance), which clearly does damage to the notion of productive-force sufficiency, one could hold (and this is closer to Marx's view) that for any combination of productive forces and relations of production, there is some further development of the productive forces which suffices for a change in production relations. Just what this development is would be a matter for empirical research to determine.

This connects with the first of the two claims distinguished above, since Marx was certainly committed to the *necessity* of productive-force change for any such production-relation variation. For these alterations, superstructural factors cannot be held essentially responsible. Thus, claim (1) instructs one to look for changes in the productive forces to explain changes in the relations of production. Without progress in the productive forces the relations of production would not be susceptible to improvement—nor would there be an impetus for change. This assertion is subject to the reservation that Marx and Engels occasionally allow for superstructural phenomena to gain (some) independence from the economic base and to react back on the relations of production, modifying them.[10] While such formulae are far from unambiguous, it is clear that they envisioned these modifications as occurring only within prescribed limits—prescribed, that is, by the productive forces. Thus, while alterations in the relations of production are not *always* a (direct) result of productive force changes, this is the case both in general and for any substantial relational mutation; accordingly, the productive forces bear the explanatory burden in Marx's theory.

Why the Productive Forces Reign

In *The German Ideology* and elsewhere Marx and Engels reflect on the considerations underlying their materialist conception of history; unfortunately, the arguments which they offer in its support are frequently flimsy and perfunctory. That material production is the "real premise" of human existence,[11] that men must eat and have shelter before they can pursue politics and philosophy,[12] hardly shows the explanatory primacy of that realm. Only a conviction that the explanatory hegemony of material production over the other provinces of social life was obvious could have blinded them to the inadequacy of such an inference.

Despite these occasional lapses in their standard of argumentation, Marx and Engels at least attempted to explicate and defend their general view of history. By contrast, they make no case for their belief in the determining role of the productive forces within the socially fundamental domain of material production. Although they often assert that production relations do change as a consequence of the growth of the productive forces, they drop only clues as to why this should be so. One might suppose that they simply perceived this as an empirical regularity and thus sought no further explanation; yet this seems unlikely. Marx certainly, with his rationalistic conception of science, considered that the dominance of material production was not just an empirically observed law but that its ascendancy within the social world was somehow necessary. Although, again, discussions of this by Marx and Engels are frequently unsatisfactory, one senses that they attached some sort of ontological primacy to material production, from which its explanatory weight for social science follows. Similarly, they seem, virtually, to have considered the determination exercised by the productive forces over the relations of production to have been necessarily—not contingently—true. If they were only reporting an observed regularity, they would not have (one supposes) so casually assumed, prior to sufficient investigation, that the productive forces have throughout history been determining of their production relations.

I think that Marx probably considered the productive forces' preeminence within material production to be intuitively and obviously true. This may be easier to see if one considers the alternatives—within his general perspective—to productive-force determinism. First, the relations of production could be determined by either superstructural or eclectic factors; second, the relations of production could be self-developing; or finally, the relations of production and the productive forces could be mutually determining. The first option clearly undermines the explanatory role of material production. The economic relations of society are supposed to structure the social world in general;

if the relations of production themselves are ruled by non-basic factors, in what sense could the former be said to be more primary? Systematic determination of the economic structure by certain non-basic factors or relations clearly counters the fundamental thrust of Marx's theory. Even to admit that relations of production are influenced by a variety of different kinds of considerations (perhaps varying in different historical situations), while it might still allow some methodological justification for viewing the relations of production as the starting point of any historical or sociological investigation, does dampen the spirit of Marx's program as well. Consistent with the primacy of material production, nothing else but the productive forces could be determining of the relations of production, and this may well be why Marx seems to assume the truth of productive-force determinism.

Of course, the relations of production could be self-determining. This second alternative is suggested by Marxian talk of the unfolding of contradictions within the relations of production, and in a sense the crises and problems of mature capitalism (for example) are for Marx inherent in capitalist relations themselves. However, the relations of production do not develop as a result of some internal, independent economic evolution. Why should they develop at all? Why do their "inherent contradictions" only become insoluble at a certain point in time? Only changes in the productive forces, only the development of man's productive capacity, permit his production relations to progress (which development allows the latter's contradictions to emerge). If man's productive ability did not expand during a given socioeconomic epoch, then—quite plainly for Marx—his relations of production will not proceed to a higher level.

The third possibility—that the productive forces and relations of production are mutually determining—enjoys some currency among contemporary Marxists. (One supposes that because they cannot bring themselves to ratify productive-force determinism, they are reluctant to impute it to Marx.) Nonetheless, such a thesis has no textual support. It goes explicitly against the passages cited at the beginning of the chapter and implicitly against the whole grain of Marx's thinking, by prohibiting historical materialism from offering a general, theoretical explanation of why any economic structure occurs when it does. Marx believes that the introduction of new relations of production is contingent on the development of the productive forces in a way in which those forces are not dependent on the relations. Why Marx should hold this position is not obvious, but it does derive from his general conception of production—to which I shall return presently.

First, though, what are the more positive reasons for Marx's theorem that the productive forces determine their relations of production? After all, why should men be thought to bring their socioeconomic relations into harmony with their expanding productive forces? Marx offers two interlaced answers to this query. First, he writes:

Men never relinquish what they have won. . . . [Thus] in order that they may not be deprived of the result attained and forfeit the fruits of civilization, they are obliged, from the moment when their mode of carrying on commerce no longer corresponds to the productive forces acquired, to change all their traditional social forms.[13]

A belief that men will or do change their social relations of production in order to accommodate existing or prospective productive forces—that men will not surrender productive advances—does seem to be a postulate about human nature. Marx, no doubt, believed it to be a patently true one and would have wished to distinguish it from more "speculative" claims about the human condition. It appears in his work as a broad socio-historical, slightly teleological, generalization about the human species as the subject of the historical process, and not as a rule applying to individual behavior.

Secondly, when a society's productive forces conflict with its relations of production, the fundamental economic equilibrium, which previously characterized it, is disrupted. This may arise, for example, because certain individuals or classes attempt to take advantage of the potential or existing productive forces at society's command (consider the seminal, capitalistic entrepreneur in the Middle Ages), or because the dominant class itself (consider the mature bourgeoisie) has loosed productive forces beyond its control. The economic disequilibrium rocks the rest of society's relations and greatly strengthens the impulse to harness the productive forces satisfactorily. Since Marx believes that society will not sacrifice its acquired productive forces, it follows for him that only the adjustment of the relations of production in order to accommodate them will allow society to restabilize.

Marx's ratiocination here purports to show why the relations of production correspond to the expanding productive forces; it does not demonstrate that these relations are not also determined by other (say, ideological) factors. Marx asserts this, but he does not argue it directly. He did believe that novel relations of production cannot be formed unless the prerequisites of those relations—the appropriate productive forces—exist. This is easy to see with regard to work relations, but Marx also held it to be true of ownership relations of production. Capitalism cannot be introduced unless the requisite development of production has taken place, even if its other preconditions are present: classical Rome is Marx's usual example of this. Similarly, he and Engels thought that the abolition of class distinctions was only possible at a certain high level of development of the productive forces. Without a sufficient level of productivity, communal production relations would only result in stagnation and decline in the mode of production—from which class distinctions would reemerge.[14] A critic, even if he accepted this, might argue that given an adequately high level of the productive forces, certain superstructural elements are still necessary for a change in production relations. In a sense, Marx would agree with this, but he avers that the presence of those other factors stems from the existence of the new productive forces. The emergence of these forces (and, one supposes, men's consciousness of this) both stimulates and makes possible the introduction of new relations of production.

The development of production relations for Marx, then, is contingent upon change in man's productive forces, and it has been suggested why such change should prompt relational adjustments. But do not the productive forces also depend upon the relations of production? Do not the relations determine the forces of production as well? Such questions, perhaps, motivate the mutual determination thesis mentioned above. Of course, the productive forces "depend" on the relations of production which utilize them, because production cannot take place outside of production relations, but this does not imply that the production relations determine the productive forces.

While the productive forces improve naturally through the activity of men (although this headway may be gradual), their progress may be stimulated to a greater or lesser extent by the existing relations of production. Different social formations, characterized by different modes of production, encourage the expansion of the productive forces to varying degrees, but acknowledging this does not subvert the thesis of productive-force determinism. Modern industry is the product of an already established capitalism, but the modern productive forces which it introduces require and ensure the realization of socialized production relations. Moreover, that production relations come to pass which have this characteristic of prompting rapid productive force advancement is itself a response to the previously existing level of productive development. Far from it embarrassing Marx that the relations of production stimulate the productive forces, he can, in fact, be called the originator of the thesis that the particular relations of production which evolve do so precisely because they are best suited, historically, to accommodate the continued development of the productive forces.

The ascendancy of the productive forces which Marx envisions flows from his image of material production itself. The production and reproduction of the prerequisites of human existence constitute the fundamental function of social organization. As a result of this on-going productive process, man's productive powers increase. While the productive forces are obviously influenced by extraneous (non-productive force) factors, they provide the clearest index of man's productive progress, of the extent of his mastery of nature, and it is this development which is of prime significance to Marx.

This productive advance, this expansion of the productive forces independent of the social form of production, Marx seems to take as a given. For him this development is a natural occurrence, implied by the very nature of human productive activity: "Every productive force is an acquired force, the product of former activity."[15] He neither queries why this is so nor seeks more primary factors to explain how it is possible that the productive forces may advance. But as a result of incessant productive progress, man's social relations of production are forced to develop. While Marx does not reduce history to the record of techological change, he does allow human history to be integrated with natural history through this developing dialectic of man's material encounter with the world around him.

Nevertheless, some have searched for an element more fundamental than the productive forces, which could either be systematically determining of those forces or explain, more generally, productive progress. Plekhanov appears to have thought that geography was such a factor.[16] Such a view, however, could not be judged an accurate rendering of Marx's theory; the passages which discuss geography in Marx's writings do not bear such a reading.[17] Although geographical conditions are very important in mankind's early development, they evolve too slowly to be considered determining of the productive forces. In addition, most geographical features (coal reserves, rivers, soil, climate) fall within the productive forces themselves. Critics like Karl Federn, on the other hand, have charged that Marx overlooked "intelligence" or some other human capacity which, it is alleged, is more fundamental than the productive forces and, in fact, their determinant.[18] Since human knowledge and productive intelligence are already built into Marx's conception of the productive forces, Federn's criticism withers. The reason one cannot look beyond the productive forces for Marx is that one cannot look beyond material production for a more solid foundation for the investigation of human society. The cycle of production and reproduction is inescapable, but man, unlike other animals, does not rest with a constant mode of subsistence. Rather, human production itself involves the expansion of his productive capacities.[19] Thus, for Marx the development of the productive forces is tied up with the very nature of production in a way in which he thought the evolution of production relations was not; the relations change only in response to the possibilities opened up by man's improving productive abilities.

Materialism and Explanation in History

To probe productive-force determinism is the purpose of the present chapter, but to facilitate this the nature of Marx's study of the relations of production and their place within the larger framework of historical materialism must be discussed.

Nowadays it is rarely asserted that "materialistic" motivation (in the lay sense in which "materialistic" is contrary to spiritual or intellectual pursuits) is any part of Marx's theory of history. Indeed the predominance of economic considerations (in the narrow sense of governing individual behavior) would seem in his conceit to be limited to market societies, or at least to capitalist ones. However, while this crude notion of the "material" in historical materialism has passed away, Marx's perspective is still frequently confused with a narrow economic determinism. This theory states, in essence, that economic variables are entirely determining of history; other social factors and relations do not interact with them and are simply puppets of economic relations. Full reality is accorded to the economic realm only while the state, laws, consciousness, et cetera, possess varying lesser degrees of substantiality. This theory is surely false, and Marx did not subscribe to it; it can hardly be thought to be compatible with the spirit of his work. Although this misinterpretation of historical materialism is perennial, it has been repeatedly corrected so the point need not be belabored here. I would only observe that the famous letters written by Engels late in his life on the materialist conception of history, however unsatisfactory they may be from the point of view of a correct and unambiguous articulation of the theory, leave no doubt that he and Marx cannot be saddled with "economic determinism" of the sort just described.[20]

From this fact it hardly follows, as some have supposed, that Marx maintained only a general interactionist viewpoint, in which no greater accent can be laid on any one factor than another. True, it is admitted, Marx studied economic relations above all, but only to give them their due in a social system in which everything interacts with everything else. Although an emphasis on the interrelatedness of all aspects of social reality has German idealist and historicist antecedents, it accords comfortably with much of the vague functionalist and structuralist sentiment of the twentieth century. Such an interpretation of Marx has the advantage of making his theory acceptable to everyone, but it dilutes it entirely too much. In answering the criticism

that the mode of production determines the character of the social, political, and intellectual life generally . . . for our own times, in which material interests preponderate, but not for the middle ages, in which Catholicism, nor for Athens and Rome, where politics reigned supreme,

Marx writes:

This much, however, is clear, that the middle ages could not live on Catholicism, nor the ancient world on politics. On the contrary it is the mode in which they gained a livelihood *that explains why* here politics, and there Catholicism, played the chief part.[21]

Despite the colorful non sequitur Marx brandishes in explaining why the mode of production determines the general organization of society, it is transparent that he believes not only that societies form integrated totalities but that these functionally related social wholes are determined by their economic base. Economic considerations are not the only force in historical events, but the manner in which the economic sphere structures the social world explains to a large extent why men's motives were what they were. The crusades in the eleventh century were not epiphenomena of feudal production relations, but for Marx those relations hold the key to understanding a world in which religious crusades were possible.

If Marx is then attempting to occupy the middle ground between a facile interactionism and a crude economic materialism —by presenting a picture of the social world in which, amongst various factors, the socioeconomic factor predominates—this moots the whole issue, which has troubled Marxists since Engels, of the precise connection between the base and the superstructure. A satisfactory reconnoitering of this labyrinthine terrain is beyond the scope of this essay. On the one hand, the question is not one of delineating some special type of determinism (such as "structural causality") which would allow a "relatively autonomous" superstructure to be determined only "in the last instance." On the other hand, the answer is not simply that the base-superstructure connection is something which can only be understood in terms of particular cases, each studied in its full empirical richness. While Marx and Engels certainly believed that all history had, in light of their theory, "to be studied afresh," that theory was intended to do more than promote historical research. If the base-superstructure connection varies in each individual society so that it can only be brought out through case studies, then the path, which the Marxian metaphor suggests should be explored, does not lead to the disclosure of the type of regularities which would make history scientific.[22]

Marx's model ranks the spheres of social life in a hierarchy. This allows him methodologically to put aside certain realms of social existence in his investigation of more fundamental relations; but it also assumes, I would contend, that the derivative character of secondary and tertiary social realms is systematic. Accordingly, the nature of the derivation would be susceptible to scientific analysis and formulation. Laird Addis has grasped this conclusion:

Thus we can say that to assert the predominance of the economic element [within Marx's doctrine of total social interactionism] is to assert that if one were to examine all the laws of interaction and all the cross-section laws of society, he would find or be able to deduce . . . (2) some statistical parallelistic laws of the if-then type from the economic to the non-economic (e.g., Marx's analysis of ideologies) and perhaps (3) a few non-statistical parallelistic laws connecting economic to non-economic variables either in an if-then or an if-and-only-if way.[23]

I think that this is a consequence which, subject to two clarifications, Marx would have embraced. First, although Marx espied a general hierarchy among the realms of social life, the laws in question would be formulated, not just for society in general but also for each specific type of socioeconomic organization. Just as for Marx there are no substantive general laws of economic life, though each period has its own,[24] so with the connections between the economic structure and superstructural relations. It is a law for Marx that the superstructure is derived from the base, but this is a law about laws: in each social formation, more specific laws govern the precise nature of this general derivation. Engels seems to have appreciated this: "All history must be studied afresh, the conditions of existence of the *different formations* of society must be examined individually before the attempt is made to *deduce* from them the political, civil-law, aesthetic, philosophic, religious, etc. views corresponding to them."[25] Here, Engels is hardly urging the abandonment of theory for historical research.[26] Rather, the laws of superstructural derivation for each mode of production must be developed from serious study. The "Preface" theory guides one's investigation, but it is no surrogate for working out the precise, historically specific but lawful, interconnections.

Secondly, although (or rather "because") lawful regularities can be disclosed among the levels of social life, the various aspects of the social complex are not independent variables. Labriola and Plekhanov long ago inveighed against the "theory of factors," the idea that history or society is a consequence of the operation of various, autonomous social realms (such as culture or economics), in favor of a more synthetic view of social life,[27] and for this they have never been accused of undermining the "orthodox" Marxist insistence on the primacy of economic relations. Indeed, Plekhanov, at least, is one of the mainstays of that tradition. To reverse the coin, appreciation of the general inter-relatedness of the social world does not rule out the identification of causal connections within that world. Although Engels' later philosophic writings stress the "universal reciprocal action" occurring within both the natural and social domains, and deprecate "metaphysical" or static modes of thinking, he did not abandon the scientific concern for empirical regularities and laws: "Only from this universal reciprocal action do we arrive at the real causal relation. In order to understand the separate phenomena, we have to tear them out of the general interconnection and consider them in isolation, and there the changing motions appear, one as cause and the other as effect."[28] In this passage Engels is discussing nature, but he would have upheld his point for the social universe as well. While the thrust of his "dialectics" is to advocate transcending a narrow preoccupation with cause and effect toward a more embracing world-view, such a perspective must include a comprehension of the lawful regularities between phenomena.

The idea that causality within human society requires that the relevant aspects of existence be totally divorced from one another in reality is surely fallacious, but some such naive consideration seems to nourish the feeling prevalent today that it is inappropriate to discuss Marx's theory in terms of "traditional" models of causation. Ollman, for example, takes the line that Marx views the whole capitalist system, in all its economic, social, political, and ideological aspects, as an organic whole without assigning causal primacy to any single realm. This absence of causality seems to be dictated in Ollman's mind by the very organicism of Marx's outlook. Not only do Ollman and others of similar persuasion appear to operate with a billiard-ball model of cause and effect, but they make the mistake of supposing that the conceptual interrelatedness of events or social relations forbids their causal connection.[29] Marx did have a very "organic" conception of society, yet causal notions are integral to his social and historical views and to the scientific work which he believed himself to be carrying out.

Since the production relations comprising a certain mode of production would only determine the various superstructural relations compatible with it to different degrees and within varying ranges, other regularities and laws would have to be utilized if the precise nature and history of a particular society were to be scientifically explicated. The relations of production for Marx shape the social world in general, but alone they do not reveal what is unique to a given social formation. The analysis of a mode of production, although according to the "Preface" it can. be accomplished "with the precision of natural science," does not straightforwardly allow deduction of its particular manifestation in a specific social formation. With regard to *Capital*'s analysis, particular historical events are contingent—although the gap between "necessity" and "contingency" here is bridged to some extent by Marxian class analysis.

Classes are defined for Marx, it was argued earlier, by their respective connections to the productive forces within a certain type of production relation. Marx's empirical claim is that the economic position of a class determines its characteristic ideas and dispositions. If the relations of production structure the social formation in general, it is class analysis which for Marx reveals how groups of men are inclined to interpret the social world and their possibilities within it from their respective vantage points; reality "presents" itself differently to the diverse classes. In light of their (largely class-determined) perspectives of the world, then, Marxoid men make their decisions, human and fallible: the workers may or may not call the general strike, their opponents may or may not struggle resolutely, and so on. History is not a closed process, in which the foreordained has only to be acted out.

Although there is a sense in which class analysis allows Marx to narrow the gulf between the "necessary" character of production relations and the "contingent" events of history, as well as between "base" and "superstructure" (since Marx's class-categorized men dwell within both sorts of relations), a gap still remains. Perceiving society through class-struggle spectacles may or may not be a useful heuristic, but in the absence of a developed science of behavior, it hardly permits full-blown scientific explanation or prediction. Often, of course, it is the unique aspect of an individual person or event which is relevant to historical understanding. When Marx's discussion turns to a subject like Lord Palmerston's foreign policy, it is not distinctively "Marxist" at all: his account becomes decidedly journalistic and conventional. Such an analysis of a particular historical phenomenon could hardly be linked directly and immediately to the "deeper" analysis of the long-term trends of the mode of production.

If I am right, then Marx does not really attempt to explain "contingent" historical events and superstructural phenomena in the manner in which he undertakes explication of more "fundamental" socioeconomic realities. His theory, essentially, simply provides him with the license to study these realities in abstraction from second- and third-order considerations. Marx's life work was directed toward studying the necessary character of a reality very much remote from everyday events. From the point of view of this fundamental, yet abstract socioeconomic reality, much of history and many of the details of a particular social world are unpredictable; the determinism of the economic structure, to which his theory directs one's attention, is measured in decades, not days. I think that Marx and Engels, with a scientific optimism characteristic of the Victorian age, did believe that scientifically adequate explanation is in principle possible for the "contingent surface of history" in all its nuance and detail; but it is important to see that some of the laws on which such a complete explanation of history would have to draw (individual psychology, for example) are not those which are the object of historical materialism's investigation. The level of the explanations which it propounds is much higher; it affords a bird's eye, not a worm's eye, view of the historical field.[30]

Marx's presentation of the capitalist mode of production, for instance, takes place at a very high level of abstraction. England illustrates his points about capitalism, but *Capital* is not a study of England (any more than the theory of gravity is a study of the apple which fell near Newton). In his 1857 manuscript introducing the *Grundrisse*, Marx discussed the function of abstraction in political economy.* Marx fancied himself, in his study of capitalist society, to be forcing his way through a welter of empirical contingencies, complex economic forms, and phenomenal appearances to grasp the innermost connections of bourgeois society; with these apprehended, it would then be possible to work one's way up to more complicated economic categories and, eventually, to account for the economic events of everyday life. In accord with this program, *Capital* begins with the most fundamental yet abstract of relations, and gradually proceeds to more "concrete" economic phenomena and the surface categories in which these deeper relations manifest themselves to the superficial observer. Even so, with regard to a particular capitalist nation, it is not just the chapter on value which is abstract but also the more "concrete" determinations, like "price of production" and "falling rate of profit." Marx's model depicts several layers of socioeconomic reality, but all are highly theoretical compared to any actual social formation—such as England in 1860 or Germany in 1900—in which the capitalist mode of production occurs.

It is important to bear in mind that Marx examines a certain type of (ownership) relations of production in its totality, that is, insofar as it constitutes a system or mode of production, exhibiting regularities which it is the task of political economy to investigate. The systematic regularities of a mode of production for

*Grundrisse (Penguin ed.) pp. 100–108 (Dietz ed., pp. 21–28). Witt-Hansen provides the best analysis of this discussion in *Historical Materialism* (Chapter IV, section A.1). Although the structure of *Capital* and the function of abstraction within it are fascinating and important, Marxists today rather exaggerate the novelty of Marx's methodological reflections. Compare, for a relevant contrast, J. S. Mill's sophisticated discussion of the Ricardian method in his "On the Definition of Political Economy" (in Ernest Nagel, ed., *John Stuart Mill's Philosophy of Scientific Method*).

Marx are both synchronic (as in the exchange between wage-labor and capital) and diachronic (as in progressive capital accumulation). The history of any particular, individual relation of production is largely a consequence of the overall tendencies of the mode of production. If the individual relation ceases to produce, for example, this will most likely be the result of pressure by other particular relations of production, of the social character of production as a whole. Individual production relations cannot be the test of productive-force determinism; insofar as the productive forces exert pressure, they generally do so—in Marx's view—in terms of the functioning of the system as a whole.

Although the relations of production are said to correspond to the productive forces, it is the relations themselves which are the object of Marx's inquiry. First, Marx is concerned to dissect society or, more accurately, its socioeconomic anatomy, and this is composed of social relations—not productive forces. Marx studies the social world and social relations, but the productive forces are not relations. Even with regard to human labor-power, in examining it in its role as a productive force, one is disregarding its social characteristics to consider its technical aspect; rather than constituting the social world, the productive forces, viewed in themselves, are an abstraction from it.

Secondly, although the forces of production determine the relations of production, the relations are not reducible to their productive forces. The relations of production can be defined in terms of men and productive forces, but while they are not holistic in this sense, no laws of individual behavior—still less any technological laws—can generate the laws of the mode of production. Economic relations have regularities which make their investigation susceptible to rigorous, scientific analysis; abstracting from individual contingencies, the recurrent features of relations of production can be identified. The relation between wage-labor and capital, for example, is not a unique event: labor-power is employed millions of times a day, and so the invariant features of this social relation can be brought out by analysis.[31] Thus, relations of production can be the object of scientific theory in a way in which—and this is the third point—the productive forces themselves cannot be. It has been suggested that the productive forces have, in Marx's eyes, a certain developmental autonomy, but this is really in terms of a larger human disposition, rather than of a lawful necessity to the particular course of technical evolution. For Marx, man's social relations, and particularly his production relations—not the productive forces—are the building blocks of the social world and the proper object of social scientific investigation and theory.

The relations of production must be understood on their own level, not as the "effects" of the productive forces to which they correspond.* The productive forces, however, move on to the historical stage, as it were, insofar as their conflict with these relations pushes society towards new Produktionsverhältnisse. The degree of advancement of the productive forces explains why a certain set of production relations, a certain mode of production, rather than another, arises. The understanding of Marx's notion of historical development proper requires that one grasp this determining role of the productive forces, and it is to this that I shall now return.

The Productive-Force Momentum

The historical level of the productive forces determines the particular mode of production which either exists or is tending to come about. The consequence of the above discussion is that the interplay of the relations and forces of production must be visualized in terms of a theoretical model, which reveals the general mode(s) of extracting surplus in a certain social formation. While the characteristics of a particular mode of production are crucial for understanding historical change, the propellent of that evolution does not simply lie in the unfolding of latent contradictions within the relations of production themselves. Rather, the momentum which pushes history ahead results from

---

*"Political economy," writes Marx, "is not technology." *Grundrisse* (Penguin ed.), p. 86.

the alternating conflict and correspondence of the relations of production and productive forces. Of course, the nature of this dialectic varies in each historical transformation with the nature of the mode of production itself, but the point here is that relations of production only evolve toward higher ones because of the expansion of society's productive capacity. The various scenarios, put forward by Marx, of this governing historical dialectic will be explored in later chapters, but the "Preface" does offer a few insights into its general character.

First, if a social order is destroyed, then all the productive forces for which it suffices (*für die sie weit genug ist*) have been developed. Read appropriately in a non-tautological sense, this ascribes to each socioeconomic order a determinate productive-force potential, a maximum level of productive development.[32] Within the context of the "Preface," this claim implies that only with the attainment of this productive level do the productive forces enter into serious conflict with the relations of production.

Secondly, if new superior relations of production replace older ones (here again, Marx is talking in terms of an entire social formation), then their material conditions have already matured within the womb of the old order. By "material conditions" Marx may be presumed to mean new productive forces, the sprouting of new production relations, or the elements necessary for the formation of either. The same developments which drive the productive forces into conflict with their relations sponsor the new relations which are to resolve this discord.

Thirdly, the socioeconomic evolution of man is marked by discernible modes of production, distinct social orders whose evolution, broadly speaking, repeats the following pattern: (a) harmony between the productive forces and relations of production turns increasingly to dissonance as society's productive capacity expands; (b) explosion is inevitable and is resolved in favor of the productive forces, which gain the relations appropriate to them; (c) equilibrium is established at a higher level. The idea that historical progress is characterized by the rise and decline of modes of production, however, is not implied by the thesis of productive-force determinism alone. Nevertheless, if the production relations which have arisen because of their appropriateness in harnessing the forces of production are protected by a class with an interest in preserving this arrangement, then it becomes more reasonable for Marx to infer that these relations will endure beyond the period of their productive-force compatibility; thus some plausibility is lent to the "Preface" model of antagonism, overthrow, and stabilization.

Finally, the "Preface" lists the major stages or epochs in mankind's advance, and the several historical transformations which these involve shall be examined later in this book. It does seem likely, though, that Marx would have been willing to revise his particular tabulation of historical periods (at least the pre-feudal ones) because he did not devote that much effort to their elaboration, and indeed his account of their economic evolution, as well be seen later, is less than satisfactory. Less likely is that Marx would have foregone the notion that historical evolution proceeds through definite socioeconomic types, definite modes of production, whose development under the sway of productive-force expansion leads to the introduction of their respective successors.

Ownership relations are grouped by Marx into a few main categories, each of which is characterized by a definite system of production, a particular socioeconomic mode of production. Within this social frame, work relations of production are frequently modulated to accommodate productive-force developments. These relations must adjust periodically in order to harness successfully the development of society's productive capacities. The given ownership relations may facilitate this, or they may be under pressure to evolve—either to allow the necessary work relations, or to correspond to already changed work relations. Thus an alteration of the social form of the economic structure itself may be required if the work relations appropriate to the productive forces are to obtain.

As a discrepancy arises between the productive forces and the work relations which are realizable within a certain set of production relations, or as a conflict waxes between new work relations and the type of ownership relation in which they are attempting to function, pressure swells for a change of the general mode of production itself.[33] This may happen through class struggle, because in their relations of production men divide into classes with different material concerns. Further, for Marx the class which represents the production relations appropriate to the level of the productive forces enjoys historical superiority: only its interest is served by initiating relations of production which are compatible with the exigencies of the emerging productive forces, and only its rule will result in a stabilized economic structure. "The conditions under which definite productive forces can be applied, are the conditions of the rule of a definite class of society."[34]

The struggle of classes over an impending mode of production projects an image of historical intentionality which history's actors do not always possess.* Men often adjust their mode of production without a complete comprehension of what they are actually doing. Indeed, the proletariat is the first class in Marx's theory to alter the mode of production while fully conscious of its historical role (thanks, in part, to the role of the theory itself). By contrast, the bourgeoisie thought they were making their revolution for liberty and equality when, according to Marx, they were in fact consolidating capitalism.

Man's relations of production are continually growing and developing in response to his productive forces, although only in specific periods do these productive forces openly conflict (in economic crisis or class struggle) with the particular type of ownership relation which characterizes the economic structure. This leads to the establishment of relations which accord more satisfactorily with the existing development of the productive forces

---

*See Engels to Sombart, March 11, 1895: "According to Marx's views all history up to now, in the case of big events, has come about unconsciously, that is, the events and their further consequences have not been intended."

and their continued expansion. The new order of production relations reshapes the skeleton of society and, as a consequence for Marx, (re)molds to different degrees the rest of society's relations. The particular dynamic of productive forces and relations of production, within the basic historical push toward higher socioeconomic forms which accompanies the continual improvement of man's productive capacity, requires for its full elucidation a theory of the particular modes of production involved.

That such a theory is very abstract with regard to any particular society can easily be illustrated by Marx's view of the transition from capitalism to socialism, which will be discussed in the next chapter. Marx presents the evolution of capitalism considered in abstraction from the specific physiognomy of any particular capitalist nation-state. *Capital* underwrites the claim that socialism is "inevitable," but by the same token it does not empower one to predict the arrival of socialism at any particular time or place—but only to affirm that the tendency of capitalist development is such as to bring it about. Clearly, the prediction or explanation of a specific socialist revolution requires more than a knowledge of the lawful workings of the capitalist system and of the inclination of the working class toward socialism (such knowledge would be necessary, of course, but hardly sufficient). That the revolution breaks out in a particular place for specific ("local") causes, however, does not sabotage the larger determinism of the productive forces.

For Marx's theory to be corroborated, it would suffice to show that the general course of historical development is shaped by the expansion of man's productive forces. The particular development of each social formation is not simply a repetition of the general theoretical interactions between productive forces and relations of production: every social group on the globe is not fated to tread through the same four or five stages of economic development, nor is the evolution of any particular social formation solely a matter of internal productive events. The "Preface" lists the general stages in the socioeconomic evolution of mankind as a whole—not the steps which history obliges every nation, without exception, to climb.* Societies rarely exist in isolation; the productive advances of one echo through the others. Marx hardly believed that the historical development of any country was strictly the outgrowth of productive-force development internal to it alone. Nation-states can skip economic stages. Why they are able to do so, however, must be explained in terms of the overall pattern of historical evolution, and the motor for that development is the productive forces.

Nations can also lag behind or even reverse course. But when one takes the difficult case of the sixteenth-century resurgence of feudal relations (in parts of eastern Europe) or of Germany's backward economic position in the early nineteenth century, the theory does not oblige one to point to the level of the productive forces alone. Rather, a Marxist analysis would have to discuss the interlocking of the advance of the productive forces with the different modes of production in those societies, as well as how the functioning of their various economic relations—and the concomitant struggle between classes—was influenced by the economic motion of the surrounding states. The restrengthening of feudal relations in response to the establishment of capitalism elsewhere would not necessarily reflect a decline in the productive forces of those countries but rather a change in the variables affecting the dialectic between productive forces and relations of production: for example, feudal relations might temporarily harness the productive forces better than a weak capitalist system exposed to external competition. The basic Marxist analysis proceeds with the study of a mode of production as an ideal type, but in any particular historical instance this mode will be functioning alongside other modes of production—both in and outside that particular society. Bringing

---

*When Marx tells the German reader of *Capital* (p. 8) that "de te fabula narratur," he is not contradicting this. The laws whose "tendencies [work] with iron necessity towards inevitable results" hold for any society in which capitalist relations of production have achieved, or are on their way to achieving, hegemony in the economic structure. That the laws of capitalism are inexorable, however, does not imply that history compels every nation to follow the capitalist road.

into consideration the reciprocal action of multiple modes of production, perhaps of different types, and their connection to the expansion of the productive forces complicates the picture, but only such an analysis can link the abstract investigation of ideal modes of production with the specific economic development of a particular nation. (Marx, it should be noted, never presented more than an explanatory sketch of the particular socioeconomic course of any individual nation's evolution.)

Since the productive forces provide the underlying rhythm to historical progress, Marx can be seen to be tendering a "technological-determinist" account of history, but this label has rather unhappy connotations. The reason for this is that those who have identified Marx's theory as one of technological determinism have offered inappropriate expositions of it. Such explications have made Marx's theory appear implausible, generally speaking, by omitting labor-power (skill, knowledge, experience) from the productive forces or by attempting to apply it directly to particular, individual alterations in the productive forces or relations of production. Because such renderings have appeared so untenable, friends of Marx have frequently adopted the position that Marx did not really intend that the productive forces be construed as determining of the relations of production. Since I have already presented a coherent (albeit abstract) account of how the productive forces determine the relations of production, there is no need to dwell further on such misformulations of historical materialism. However inadequately, Marx's "deterministic" expounders have at least underlined the fact that Marx did see the growth of the productive forces as the prime mover of social development. The linking of this with particular social forms and the struggle between classes constitutes what is peculiar to his perspective.

Now the exact manner in which a given set of ownership relations, a particular mode of production, is made necessary by the level and nature of productive development must be traced concretely for each historical period if Marx's theory of history is to be fully understood. Accordingly, I turn from these general reflections to the investigation of the specific transitions which Marx discussed: first, the passage from capitalism to socialism, which was the main object of his life's theoretical work; and second, the evolution of previous world history through several distinct modes of production. These studies should allow the nature of the dynamic between productive forces and relations of production, the driving force of historical change and development, to be explicated more concretely. The fruits of this inquiry, with regard to the general understanding of Marx's materialist conception of history, will be harvested in the last chapter.

CHAPTER THREE

From Capitalism to Socialism

I N T H E P R E C E D I N G chapters the character of the productive forces and of the relations of production has been investigated at length, and the nature of their conjunction in Marx's theory of historical change has been presented. The task of this chapter is to trace Marx's analysis of a specific historical transformation in terms of this previous discussion.

In the "Preface" to *A Contribution to the Critique of Political Economy*, which will again serve as a guide, Marx wrote:

> At a certain stage of development, the material productive forces of society come into conflict with the existing relations of production or—what is but a legal expression for the same thing—with the property relations within the framework of which they have operated hitherto. From forms of development of the productive forces these relations turn into their fetters. Then begins an era of social revolution.

Since Marx devoted his major theoretical efforts to the study of the capitalist mode of production, it is not surprising that capitalism is generally understood to be the paradigmatic exemplification of the "Preface" motif. Yet, it is not immediately clear how Marx's lengthy and rich descriptions of the nature and tendency of capitalist development fit the pithy formulation of the "Preface." Marx undoubtedly believed that they did, but his economic work was unfinished, and loose ends exist. To explicate Marx's account of capitalism in terms of the discrepancy between the productive forces and the relations of production, which he hypothesizes above, will be the main concern of this chapter.

I shall first outline the developmental tendencies of capitalism as it is discussed in the premier volume of *Capital* and then go on to show that Marx's presentation there does not suffice to unravel the "Preface," but requires that the fuller corpus of his writings be interrogated. The second part of this chapter treats of the arrival of socialism, but despite the familiarity of some of the themes upon which I shall touch, the acquisition of socialism is rarely situated accurately within Marx's "Preface" perspective.

The Tendencies of Capitalist Development
The "Preface" Conflict and the First Volume of Capital

The very nature of capitalist production, spurred on as it is by competition, necessitates that it be on an expanding scale—that is, that at least part of the surplus produced by capital be converted into new capital and reemployed.[1] This is, of course, synonymous with capital accumulation. With capital's reproduction on a progressive scale, the proletariat increases: "more capitalists or larger capitalists at this pole, more wage-workers at that."[2] Since this growth of capital augments the demand for labor, when the customary supply of labor is surpassed, wages rise, and the condition of the wage laborers is somewhat ameliorated. Such an increase in wages can (at best) decrease the amount of unpaid labor which the worker is obligated to supply, but this reduction can never reach the point at which it would threaten the whole system. If the increase blunts the stimulus of gain, then accumulation slackens, lessening the disproportion between capital and exploitable labor-power: "The mechanism of the process of capitalist production removes the very obstacles that it temporarily creates. The price of labor falls again to a level corresponding with the needs of the self-expansion of capital."[3]

This correlation between accumulation and the rate of wages results from the very nature of capitalist accumulation, which excludes "diminution in the degree of exploitation of labor," and Marx writes that: "It cannot be otherwise in a mode of production in which the laborer exists to satisfy the needs of self-expansion of existing values, instead of, on the contrary, material wealth existing to satisfy the needs of development on the part of the laborer."[4] For Marx this is one of the major contradictions of capitalist production (a contradiction which is latent in the two aspects of a commodity, namely use-value and exchange-value), and it signifies for him the futility of all attempts to reform capitalism, because such efforts necessarily preserve the basic character of the capital-labor relation. At the same time this "coercive relation, which compels the working-class to do more work than the narrow round of its own life-wants prescribes,"[5] provides the historical justification for capitalism since it allows for the tremendous increase of man's productive power, of his control over nature, which will provide the material foundation for socialism.[6]

In the evolution of the capitalist system, the enhanced productivity of social labor becomes the most powerful lever of accumulation; this expanding productiveness expresses itself in the growth of the means of production relative to the labor-power combined with them. The different capitals are in competition and do battle by cheapening their respective commodities, a process which hinges largely on the productiveness of labor and the scale of production. The larger capitalists beat the smaller ones, and thus centralization completes the work of accumulation by enabling the surviving industrial capitalists to extend their scale further. "Everywhere the increased scale of industrial establishments is the starting-point for a more comprehensive organization of the collective work of many, for a wider development of their material motive forces."[7]

The increasing size of industrial enterprises (the "concentration" of capital) and the amalgamation of previously independent capitals ("centralization") become a source of new alterations in the composition of capital, accelerating the decline of its variable (as compared with its constant) constituent. Two movements are apparent: first, in the course of accumulation fewer laborers are attracted in proportion to the magnitude of capital, and second, the original capital periodically changes composition, expelling laborers formerly employed by it. As a result of capitalist accumulation, reasons Marx, a relatively redundant population is created, a population greater than suffices for the average need of capital's self-expansion. While capitalist accumulation increasingly demands more labor-power, this is at a diminishing rate—a rate which is below the pace of the population growth which it stimulates. Marx calls this capital's "relatively shrinking need for an increasing population."[8]

Despite the problematic support for his claim that under capitalism "a surplus laboring population is a necessary product of accumulation," Marx is more concerned to emphasize that "this surplus-population becomes, conversely, the lever of capitalist accumulation, nay, a condition of existence of the capitalist mode of production."[9] The "industrial reserve army" which is formed by the surplus population is a mass of human material which can be thrown into production, according to the needs of capital expanding into new areas, without injury to the scale of production in other areas. Capitalist production, Marx believes, cannot rely on the disposable labor-power which the natural increase of population yields; it also requires this industrial reserve (which it creates) of potential laborers. Both the existence and the employment of the surplus population follow the sinusoid of capitalist development, and the industrial cycle itself "depends on the constant formation, the greater or less absorption, and the re-formation" of the reserve labor army.[10] Not only does capitalist accumulation spawn an excess population; the production of that surplus population is a necessary component of modern industry and a condition of its existence.

Capitalism operates under two opposing tendencies: on the one hand, it constantly reduces the labor-time necessary for the production of commodities; on the other hand, it attempts to appropriate the greatest quantity of surplus labor. At a given level of productivity, maximizing surplus labor is possible only by hiring more laborers: "It is therefore equally a tendency of capital to increase the laboring population, as well as constantly to posit a part of it as surplus population—population which is useless until such time as capital can utilize it."[11] Capitalist production, in sum, both requires and promotes the growth of the laboring population, while continually creating an artificial overpopulation.

The general movement of wages is regulated by the expansion and contraction of the reserve army, following shifts in the industrial cycle. The enforced idleness of one part of the working population forces the other part to overwork (which, in turn, may permit the number of employed laborers to fall).[12] In periods of both stagnation and prosperity, the industrial reserve army weighs down the active labor force: it is the "pivot upon which the law of demand and supply of labor works." This consummates the despotism of capital and rivets the Prometheus of labor to the rock of capital.[13]

The increasing quantity of means of production which can be set in motion by a progressively diminishing expenditure of labor-power means in capitalism that "the higher the productiveness of labor, the greater is the pressure of the laborers on the means of employment, the more precarious, therefore, becomes their condition of existence."[14] As capital accumulates, the lot of the laborers grows worse because the raising of social productivity is brought about at the individual's expense: the means of production are the means of his exploitation, he becomes a mere appendage of the machine, his work is made mean and is estranged from the intellectual powers of the labor process, his life becomes work time, and his wife and child, too, are dragged "beneath the wheels of the Juggernaut of capital."[15] At the same time, the industrial reserve army increases, and with it a surplus population "whose misery is in inverse ratio to its torment of labor."[16]

Since Marx says that the condition of the worker deteriorates "be his payment high or low," he probably has relative, rather than absolute impoverishment in mind (as well as an intensification of noneconomic misery). This change from some of his earlier writings reflects his recognition that a decline in the laborers' share in the total value product may be accompanied by an increase in the use-values which they receive.[17] In Marx's account, however, the relative impoverishment of the employed laborers is accompanied by absolute bankruptcy for increasing numbers of unemployed workers. Accumulation of wealth at one pole corresponds with an accumulation of misery at the other.[18] This is the general law of capitalist accumulation, illustrated by *Capital* with fifty pages of censuring reports and statistics.

In the penultimate chapter of the first volume of *Capital*, Marx explains that the expropriation of the capitalists shall be "by the action of the immanent laws of capitalistic production itself, by the centralization of capital," and he reviews the productive fruits which accompany this process of centralization.[19] But, as has been shown, along with these advances "grows the mass of misery, oppression, slavery, degradation, exploitation." At the same time, Marx introduces the working class, whose revolt ripens with capital's accumulation: its members are "disciplined, united, organized by the very mechanism of the process of capitalist production itself." The passage which Marx quotes there from the *Communist Manifesto* underscores his allegiance to the tenet that the proletariat is the active force, the "really revolutionary class," the gravedigger of capitalism, who will carry through its expropriation.

Marx characterizes this historical process in two ways. First:

The monopoly of capital becomes a fetter upon the mode of production. . . . Centralization of the means of production and socialization of labor at last reach a point where they become incompatible with their capitalist integument. This integument is burst asunder.

And then, secondly, he writes that capitalist private property

is the first negation of individual private property, as founded on the labor of the proprietor. But capitalist production begets, with the inexorability of a law of Nature, its own negation. It is the negation of negation.[20]

The last sentences are quite famous, but they are only a catchy way of describing the historical tendency of capitalism, not an explanation of it. What is important, however, is what exactly capitalism begets and why. It seems, then, that the first formulation offers a better thumbnail explanatory sketch, but can either account be understood as representing fully the conflict between the productive forces and the relations of production, as postulated in the "Preface"? I think not.

The glaring contradiction of the capitalist system as it is displayed by Marx in the first volume of *Capital* is that this mode of production necessarily generates enormous productive power and immense social wealth for a few while increasing (or, at the very least, perpetuating) the misery of the mass of society. Earlier this was characterized as a contradiction between use-value and exchange-value or, more generally, between capitalist production and social needs. This is all the sharper because the labor process itself has been socialized and centralized, while exchange and appropriation are still individual.[21] Society is producing a social product, the bulk of which is being appropriated by a dwindling number of capitalists.

Marx does declare that the monopoly of capital fetters the mode of production, but this differs from the fettering of the productive forces which is specified by the "Preface." The mode of production in this volume of *Capital* is fettered in the sense that production is not properly fulfilling its function (which is, after all, the satisfaction of society's needs) because of its particular social form. This, however, has characterized capitalism— although perhaps not so dramatically—since its earliest days. Accordingly, this fettering of the mode of production may be distinguished from a restriction on the development of the productive forces themselves (which, on the contrary, have been expanded and increased by capitalism). So far in Marx's account, the productive forces have not been restrained but are growing continually in productivity and scale. They are not hampered or standing idle, nor has the productive process been clogged.

Capitalism has sacrificed the humanity of the producers and the well-being of society in its quest for greater and greater surplus-value but not (it appears) the augmentation of the productive forces. The forms of development of the productive forces do not seem to have turned, as the "Preface" states, into fetters on those forces.

Against the above, it might be contended that the increasing social imbalance generated by capitalism's simultaneous production of wealth and misery, described in the first volume of *Capital*, is just what Marx meant by the conflict between productive forces and relations of production, and that to demand that the productive forces per se—rather than their social employment— be shown to be hindered is inappropriately literal.[22]

There is in fact some textual support for such an assertion. For example, in a speech in 1856 Marx contrasts the impressive growth of the productive forces under capitalism with the horrors of wage-slavery without suggesting that capitalist relations may balk the development of the productive forces themselves. He appears to equate the former opposition with the contradiction between the productive forces and relations of production: "This antagonism between modern industry and science on the one hand, modern misery and dissolution on the other hand; this antagonism between the productive powers, and the social relations of our epoch, is a fact."[23]

Rather than argue directly against the proposal to interpret the "Preface" loosely, I intend to show that Marx did in fact hold that the productive forces were fettered by their capitalist relations in a strict sense, and that it is this conflict which grounds the contradiction with which the first volume is concerned. A fuller account will emerge from Marx's posthumous economic writings, which allows the "Preface" scenario to be unpacked—at least in terms of Marx's vision of the transformation of capitalism into socialism.

Finally, it needs mentioning that the conflict between the productive forces and relations of production should not be equated with the opposition between workers and capitalists, as it has been by many commentators.[24] Earlier I rejected the claim that the revolutionary proletariat is itself part of the productive forces, and indeed the "Preface" conflict, unlike the war between proletarians and bourgeoisie, also marks economic structures prior to capitalism. The class struggle in any social formation is distinct from the contradiction between the development of the productive forces and their social integument, which paves the way for a new social stage. The antagonism between workers and bosses is intrinsic to capitalism—not the product of its expansion of the productive forces, as the "Preface" demands. The "Preface" text signals a contradiction of a different order.

The Plenary Portrayal

While the first volume of *Capital* does not enlarge enough on the "Preface" theme, it does hint at crises, the stagnation resulting from which would seem prima facie to involve a fettering of the productive forces. To follow this lead and to present a more complete account of Marx's view of capitalist development, it will be necessary to turn to the remainder of his mature writings on economics, the unfinished books of *Capital* and the *Grundrisse*.

As was seen above, as capitalism develops, a constant or even dwindling number of laborers is able to produce an ever-waxing wealth of commodities. The natural growth of capital implies that an increasing quantity of means of production is combined with a proportionally shrinking amount of labor-power. For Marx, it is a law of capitalist production that its development is attended by a decrease of variable capital relative to both the constant and total capital set in motion.* Since variable capital is

---

*Marx was clearly captivated by the increasing mechanization and scale of production triggered by the industrial revolution, and he thought it "an incontrovertible fact," and "self-evident or a tautological proposition," that productive development implied increased capital expenditure on machinery and raw materials, both absolutely and relative to capital expended in wages. *Theories of Surplus Value* 3: 364, 366. Even on Marx's terms the capitalist, in attempting to cheapen his costs, is indifferent, ceteris paribus, to whether the savings is in constant or variable capital, and it is likely that the twentieth century has seen improvements in the means of production and in productivity without a general change in organic composition (contrary to Marx's prediction).

the source of surplus value, this change in the composition of capital in at least the key spheres of production must induce a gradual fall in the general rate of profit. Marx, along with other nineteenth-century economists, held that this was the actual trend of capitalist production, although for Marx the fall does not manifest itself in absolute form but as a somewhat latent inclination.*

Marx's law does not rule out a growth of the absolute amount of labor consumed and, thus, a gain in the absolute volume of profit. The same causes, in fact, produce both an increasing mass of profit and a subsiding profit rate:

> The same development of the productiveness of social labor, the same laws which express themselves in a relative decrease of variable as compared to total capital . . . manifests itself, aside from temporary fluctuations, in a progressive increase of the total employed labor-power and a progressive increase of the absolute mass of surplus-value, and hence of profit.[25]

This twofold movement represents an expansion of the total capital employed at a pace more rapid than that at which the rate of profit drops, and so for Marx there is an inner and necessary connection between these two apparently contradictory propensities.

A descent in the rate of profit and accelerated accumulation both stem from the development of productiveness and reinforce each other. Accumulation hastens the fall of the profit rate, which in turn quickens the centralization of smaller capitals. Since the rate of profit is the goad of capitalist production, its decline checks the formation of new capitals and the reinvestment of old. While counteracting influences "cross and annul the effect of the general law, and . . . give it merely the characteristic of a tendency," the law still looms as a threat to the capitalist production process.[26] The tendency for the profit rate

*Marx refers to the concern with which English political economy, and Ricardo in particular, viewed the falling rate of profit (*Capital* 3: 242, 259). John Stuart Mill, by contrast, thought this decline—the slowing of the economy to the "stationary state"—to be a good thing (*Principles of Political Economy*, Book IV, Chapter 6).

to drop lessens stability. "It breeds over-production, speculation, crises, and surplus-capital alongside surplus-population."* While the sinking rate of profit undermines the motive of capitalist production, its specter exacerbates the frenzy of competition and production. The system overproduces commodities as capitalists fight for a share of a proportionally dwindling bounty of surplus. With the falling rate of profit, the development of the productive forces fronts a "barrier which has nothing to do with the production of wealth as such"; this barrier testifies to the historical and transitory nature of capitalism, which cannot be considered an absolute mode for the production of wealth.[27]

In addition to the direct production process in capitalism, which is the creation of surplus-value, a second act is required: the entire mass of commodities, the total product, must be sold in order for this surplus-value to be realized by the capitalist. Capitalism attempts to produce to the limit of its productive capacity without regard to the market.[28] Yet, as Marx points out: "The conditions of direct exploitation [of the laborer], and those of realizing [surplus value], are not identical. They diverge not only in place and time, but also logically."[29] This process of realization is limited by (1) the proportional relation of the various branches of production and (2) the consumer power of society. The law of value governs the former—that is, how much of society's disposable working time can be expended on each particular class of commodity—but in the anarchy of capitalist production this is only a posteriori:

The law of value of commodities ultimately determines how much of its disposable working-time society can expend on each particular class of commodities. But this constant tendency to equilibrium, of the various spheres of production, is exercised, only in the shape of a reaction against the constant upsetting of this equilibrium.[30]

Capital 3: 242, 258–59. But compare J. S. Mill, in the previous footnote. That a falling rate of profit should have such adverse consequences is nowhere near as obvious as Marx and some subsequent Marxists seem to have assumed. Why it has the consequences it does for Marx cannot be separated from problems in the process of realization, discussed below.

Because production in the various spheres is not proportionate, supply does not equal demand; in addition, overproduction in a few spheres may provoke overproduction in others.[31]

The possibility of crisis exists in the very relation of purchase and sale; accordingly, Marx rejects the "childish dogma" of Say, that every supply elicits its demand. On the contrary, the metamorphosis of commodities in exchange is the unity of two processes—a unity which is manifest when they become independent of each other in crisis.[32] In an economy where money is not just a means to the exchange of goods but is the object of that exchange, the sale of goods is easily separable from the purchase of others, thus raising the specter of crisis (since crisis issues from the inability to sell). The fact that in reality one is dealing with the intertwining of many different capitals only heightens the likelihood of crisis. This is further intensified by the use of money as a means of payment, that is, with the development and extension of credit; when the same sum of money functions in a whole series of reciprocal transactions and obligations, the inability to pay, when it occurs, strikes not only at one, but at many points.[33] As a result, most industrial and commercial crises assume the form of monetary crises.[34] Marx emphasizes that he is just explaining the possibility of crisis, its general form, and not its cause. So far, the cause has been shown to rest on the inability of capital to be realized due to the inherent disequilibrium of a system based on competitive and private production.

Marx amplifies this in the second volume of *Capital*, which traces the interdependence of the different sectors of production and analyzes the requirements which must be satisfied if even a system of simple reproduction is to achieve equilibrium. With accumulation and reproduction on an extended scale, the danger of disequilibrium is even greater. As Marx remarks, summarizing pages of the second volume, the "process is so complicated that it offers ever so many occasions for running abnormally."[35] Perhaps the key factor in maintaining equilibrium and proportion between the spheres of production is social consumption.

Consumer power, however, does not rest on the absolute productive power of society but is "based on antagonistic conditions of distribution, which reduce the consumption of the bulk of society to a minimum."[36] It remains further restricted by the tendency of capital to accumulate, by its drive to produce surplus-value on an increasing scale. Capitalist production incessantly revolutionizes the methods of production, expands industry, and extends the market, but "the more productiveness develops, the more it finds itself at variance with the narrow basis on which the conditions of consumption rest."[37] In the third volume of *Capital* Marx writes: *"The ultimate reason for all real crises always remains the poverty and restricted consumption of the masses* as opposed to the drive of capitalist production to develop the productive forces as though only the absolute consuming power of society constituted their limit."[38] The context in which this passage appears, unfortunately, is enigmatic, and Marx was certainly far from having woven such hints into a complete theory of "underconsumption." But the basic point recurs.

In *Theories of Surplus Value*, Marx stresses that "the majority of the population, the working people, can only expand their consumption within very narrow limits," and overproduction under capitalism ensues precisely from this fact.[39] Later, in a discussion of Sismondi, Marx again identifies this as the fundamental contradiction: unrestricted development of the productive forces yielding increased wealth in the form of commodities which must be turned into cash, while the system is based on the fact that the mass of producers is restricted to necessaries.* From what was said earlier (pp. 84–85), it should be transparent that for Marx an appreciation of real wages cannot solve this prob-

---

Theories of Surplus Value 2: 534–35, 528; see *Capital* 3: 266. The point which Marx makes here does not seem to be affected, in his mind, by his simultaneous belief in the growing numbers of unproductively employed workers (in his technical sense). See *Capital* 1: 446; and *Theories of Surplus Value* 1: 201; 2: 573; 3: 63. Even if one presumes that the income of these middle classes, like that of the servant class, was limited to the value of their labor-power, their wage represents both an expenditure of capitalist revenue and an increase in the consuming power of the population (thus, reducing the likelihood of crisis due to underconsumption or lack of effective demand).

lem, since a diminution in profit is not possible in a capitalist system: "Crises are always prepared by precisely a period in which wages rise generally and the working-class actually gets a larger share of that part of the annual product which is intended for consumption."[40]

The fact that the capitalist class appropriates the surplus does not ease the contradiction of underconsumption, since the capitalist is required to accumulate and cannot consume as much surplus as is created. The problem of underconsumption—in addition to its connection with the problem of disequilibrium between the various spheres of production and consumption in an economic system which is not subject to social planning—is in part a result of capitalism's compulsion, discussed in the first volume of *Capital*, to generate wealth on the one hand and poverty on the other. In the other volumes of *Capital* this latter contradiction is closely linked with the analysis of crisis, and consequently with the fettering of the productive forces. Marx's theory of capitalist development is both a theory of accumulation and a theory of crisis.

The source of both of these limits to the realization of value is the fact that capitalism implies the accumulation of capital and the pursuit of surplus-value on an extending scale. Along with this, capital is concentrated, and the social productiveness of labor swells, manifesting itself in the increased magnitude of the already produced productive forces and the relative smallness of the capital laid out in wages. Marx identifies the underlying contradiction of capitalism as the tendency toward absolute, unconditional development of the productive forces,[41] while the aim of the system is to preserve the value of existing capital and to promote its self-expansion. The limits within which this preservation and self-expansion can move continually conflict with the method of production employed by capital for its purposes. Capitalist production strives to overcome its restrictions, and crises result.[42] "The crises are always but momentary and forcible solutions of the existing contradictions. They are violent eruptions which for a time restore the disturbed equilibrium."[43]

Existing capital is depreciated by crisis and withheld from circulation; the exchange-value as well as the use-value of the means of production and labor-power may be destroyed by their unemployment. This brakes the fall in the rate of profit, but as the cycle is renewed, the barrier to capitalist production remains, only "on a more formidable scale" since the concentration and centralization of capital has only been aided by the crisis.

The "Preface" Revisited

The analysis of the first volume of *Capital* can now be seen to have been woven by Marx into a more complete, albeit more complex, picture of the nature of capitalist development. This larger and more panoramic tableau clearly portrays the demise of capitalism from the perspective of the historic conflict between the development of the productive forces and their capitalist relations of production:

> The *real barrier* of capitalist production is *capital itself*. . . . The limits within which the preservation and self-expansion of the value of capital resting on the expropriation and pauperization of the great mass of producers can alone move—these limits come continually into conflict with the methods of production employed by capital for its purposes, which drive towards unlimited extension of production, towards production as an end in itself, towards unconditional development of the social productivity of labor. The means—unconditional development of the productive forces of society—comes continually into conflict with the limited purpose, the self-expansion of the existing capital.[44]

In light of the exposition thus far, one may appreciate that the misery begot by capitalism ("the expropriation and pauperization of the great mass of producers") is no longer simply contrasted with the system's simultaneous production of immense wealth and productive power. Of course, Volume One showed the poverty-wealth dichotomy as indissoluble, but now this couplet is perceived as betokening structural defects which, with increasing severity and regularity, undermine society's capacity to reproduce itself materially (at least in anything like the manner suggested by the nature and quality of its productive forces). Similarly, the contradiction between social production and pri-

vate appropriation now reveals more strikingly the historical un-
tenability of continued capitalist production; its dissolution no
longer appears to rest exclusively with the rise of the oppressed
against injustice.

As a result of the fact that capitalism's economic contradictions
break out essentially in the process of realization, it is not surprising that the full force of the conflict between the productive
forces and their relations should not have emerged in Volume
One of *Capital*, where (unlike Volumes Two and Three) Marx is
only concerned with the process of producing capital. Capitalism
produces both abundance and want (Volume One), but only
when its circulation (Volume Two) and production as a whole
(Volume Three) are examined are its relations of production
seen to become fetters on the development of the productive
forces.

It still remains, however, to examine more carefully how the
previous analysis (pp. 91–97) fits the "Preface" quotation with
which this chapter began. In the sentences under consideration,
the "productive forces" are said both to come into contradiction
(in Widerspruch) with the "relations of production" and to become fettered by the same. The two concepts in quotation marks
have already been discussed at length, and it will be recalled that
the productive forces do not enter the production process except in certain, definite relations of production.

It is, nonetheless, intelligible to discuss the productive forces
apart from such relations; further, any given set of productive
forces can at least hypothetically be combined into different relations, some of which might reasonably be described as more
efficient or productive than others. The productive forces in
(say) a shoe factory yield to optimum employment or utilization
in (at least) one particular relation or organization of production, and if this fails to occur (and, ex hypothesi, this failure is
not the result of technological factors), the productive forces
could be said to be "fettered." The productive forces are hampered in that they are not being utilized to their full capacities,
which would require new relations.

It is, of course, possible to speak not only of recombining a given set of productive forces in different production relations but also of employing productive forces not currently in any given relation of production. Failure to introduce or utilize available productive forces would be a "fettering" of them. To begin using a factor of production, however, which society has never before exploited, or to employ one which society previously utilized but now no longer does, would be to bring into its production relations something which could be described as having previously been a productive force only "potentially." These potential productive forces are not immaterial or ghostly things but exist just as certainly as the actually employed productive forces. Like men whose labor-power is unemployed, they exist in other capacities, roles, or relations—outside of Produktionsverhältnisse.

Whether coal is a potential productive force for the particular community in whose hills it resides depends on a whole set of empirical determinations about the nature of production in that society. It is not a matter which can be decided on the level of what is or is not a priori a productive force. Another point is related: that something is a potential productive force for a society capable of utilizing it but not doing so by no means implies that it should be introduced into production (for instance, the labor-power of a class of intellectual or religious leaders, or an outdated type of mechanical power). Such an issue hangs on considerations of a different sort. In any society there would seem necessarily to be "fettered" productive forces in this sense, because not all men, for example, would be occupied in production, or every raw material exploited. That this is the case, of course, is far from undesirable.

It may seem excessive to hold that any unused productive force is ipso facto fettered, and accordingly one might suggest that a distinction should be drawn between productive forces which are prevented from being employed (or employed in an optimal fashion) because of the specific nature of the ownership relations of production and those unemployed for other reasons. But even if such a differentiation were feasible, the trouble which prompts it is not all that pressing. Marx's concern is not that there are fettered productive forces (certainly not in the wide sense of "fettered"), but rather that the relations of production have ceased to be forms of development of the productive forces. When this occurs, these relations come both to cramp the employment of the existing productive forces (whether they languish inside or outside of production) and to restrain their further development (which includes failing to introduce new—or "potential"—productive forces which are at the command of society's technology, insofar as this would raise productivity). The fact that unused (or "fettered") productive forces exist need not mean that either event takes place.

Restricting the further development of the productive forces encompasses an additional type of fettering, not yet specifically designated, where the relations of production prevent the formation of materially possible productive forces which do not yet exist.[45] Consider, for example, a society in which the principles of steam engines and how to manufacture them are well understood, and the requisite raw materials are available, but the relations of production make their manufacture and employment impossible. This would appear to be a case of fettering, but neither of actual nor of potential productive forces in the senses discussed. Rather, the *development* of the productive forces, which in this example involves the creation of new ones, is bridled. This species of fettering appears in perfect accord with the "Preface."

A social formation, however, is not indicted by the conflict of its production relations with the progress of its productive forces (potential or otherwise) unless the fettering is widespread and salient. According to the "Preface" (see pp. 76–77 in Chapter Two), this accompanies the attainment within the old relations of production of a maximum development of the productive forces. Although this should not be interpreted over-literally, Marx, it would seem, did believe that the conflict between productive forces and relations of production would intensify with the expansion of the productive forces until any further advance was virtually thwarted. This takes place, in Marx's view, under mature capitalism: it destroys and idles productive forces, shackles them in inappropriate relations, and stints both their development and the introduction of new productive forces. The furtherance of production no longer coincides with the motion of capitalist economic relations. This is what should be understood by these relations turning from *forms* of development of the productive forces into fetters on them. This non-coincidence leads to the economic contradictions which wrench capitalism, but it does not intimate that the productive forces cease altogether to be either developed or employed by the system.

Yet, something like this would seem to have been at least implicitly attributed to Marx by those who have found a theory of complete capitalist breakdown (Zusammenbruchstheorie) in his writings or have attempted to construct such a theory from them. Despite the controversy which surrounded this issue at the turn of this century,[46] there is little in Marx to support the contention that he envisioned capitalism ending in one final economic holocaust, from the ashes of which the phoenix of socialism would spring.

Naturally Marx held that any specific capitalist society would in fact be racked by the contradictions which his theory delineates, but he would not have maintained that it would proceed acquiescently to the endpoint of those contradictions in order to be redeemed by the negation of negation. The point is not just that capitalism is prevented by the intervention of the proletariat from proceeding to its final collapse, but that there is no final contradiction followed by disintegration. Capitalism begets contradictory tendencies, which increase in strength, but it neither contains within itself the possibility of their reconciliation nor permits the final triumph of one over the other: each violent disruption only restores the disturbed equilibrium. The increasingly antagonistic propensities of capitalism render it historically untenable: they do not imply that the system must "self-destruct"—that is, that its continued existence becomes logically impossible.

At a certain stage of capitalism's development, according to

Marx, society's productive forces contravene their social relations of production. This takes the form of capitalism's driving
force—the pursuit of surplus value, spurred on by competition
—turning against itself because the means (increased productivity and concentration) used to accomplish this goal undermine
its achievement. Capitalist ownership relations provide the
framework within which the productive forces are set in motion:
they encourage their employment and development, on the one
hand, and fetter them on the other. The first is familiar and
springs from competition and the drive for profit: the rapid development and introduction of new productive forces, involving
large-scale production, scientific management, and so on.

The second follows a vignette like this. A conflict between the
actual production process as it is carried out in certain relations
of production (wherein the productive forces have been satisfactorily harnessed) and the preservation and expansion of value
emerges when the latter is threatened by the former, perhaps by
a declining rate of profit due to high wages or by the production
of commodities whose value cannot be realized. A crisis may be
generated as capitalists panic; the market drops, and capital is
destroyed. In any event, production is cut back, and stagnation
ensues as the formerly employed forces of production now lie
idle; any further advancement ceases. A discrepancy then exists
between the productive forces and the work relations, which are
forced by their capitalist integument to fetter the full utilization
and development of the productive forces.

Like regurgitation, the crisis brings relief to a distressed system: the shackles on the productive forces are loosened, and
they again enjoy fuller employment and swift expansion. Nonetheless, relief is but temporary since the system remains un-
changed, and the productive forces are continually vulnerable
to dysfunctional work relations. Under mature capitalism the
productive forces enter a position where their full contribution
to production can be achieved only by a change in the ownership
relations of production. Capitalist relations fetter the development of the productive forces and disrupt the functioning of

their work relations. It is on the field of this conflict that the nature of the transition to socialism, to which I now turn, must be examined.

The Transition to Socialism

> This transformation [from capitalism to socialism] stems from the development of the productive forces under capitalist production, and from the ways and means by which this development takes place.   —*Capital* 3: 264

So far I have tried to explain how Marx's analysis of capitalism fits the compressed account of a conflict between the productive forces and relations of production which was advanced by the "Preface"; it remains now to elucidate the character of the transition to socialism which takes place on the quaking ground of this antagonism. The productive forces should be understood as the driving force behind the historical rupture which constitutes socialism, because they provide the material basis on which new and more compatible relations of production both can and must be brought about. The productive forces are the terms of the relations which constitute the new and more stable economic structure, but they do not establish such relations themselves. In capitalism that is the job of the proletariat (and I will return to this below), but the productive forces do create conditions hospitable to social upheaval and revolution and compose the foundation for a social formation in which the productive forces are again in harmony with the relations of production. The development of the productive forces leads to a conflict with the relations of production, but it also points the way out of the contradictions of capitalism.

Joint-Stock Companies and Socialism

This relatively simple point is blurred over by Shlomo Avineri, who, by making the German word "Aufhebung" work overtime, interprets Marx as viewing capitalism's overthrow as an exercise of creative dialectic.[47] After looking for the dialectic(s) which will yield "the realization of the hidden tendencies of capitalist society itself," Avineri finds it deep in the third volume of *Capital*. Here the "cryptic Hegelian code" of Volume One's peroration— the "negation of negation" passage—is supposedly deciphered by Marx, who "specifically named the stock companies and the co-operative factories as two examples of the process through which the hidden transition from capitalism to socialism is already occurring."[48] Presumably, what Avineri has in mind with his talk of "hidden tendencies" and "internal change" (and in light of his larger theme of the not-really-revolutionary nature of Marx's thought) is that capitalism evolves of its own accord into socialism—behind the backs, as it were, of its members. This novel interpretation requires closer scrutiny, however.

To begin with the cooperative factories: Marx, although impressed by these experiments and undoubtedly seeing in them a presentiment of future production relations, considered that such projects were not the means by which socialism would be achieved. Rather, they were devices of an educational nature, demonstrating the ripeness of the productive forces for a new form of social production: "Co-operative factories furnish proof that the capitalist has become no less redundant as a functionary in production as he himself, looking down from his high perch, finds the big landowner redundant."[49] Such cooperative experiments, however, were initiated outside of the sphere of capitalist relations (hence, their "utopian" character in the classic Marxist sense). It is precisely because they are not a change internal to capitalist production (but an anomalous spin-off) that they do not provide for Marx a "transition" to socialism. To call them this, as Avineri does, is misleading.

Joint-stock companies, on the other hand, are not a "hidden transition" to socialism because they are simply a further development of capitalism, a continuation of the accumulation and centralization which has already been described.[50] Nor is the fact that ownership is separated from management responsibility unique for this is the tendency of all capital when it reaches a certain size.[51] "Instead of overcoming the antithesis between the character of wealth as social and as private wealth, the stock companies merely develop it in a new form."[52] Engels, who was particularly interested in the development of stock companies and cartels, draws attention to this by pointing out that their speedy growth intensifies the contradictions of capitalist production (overproduction, falling profits, and so on); it is presumably for this that he is rebuked by Avineri for failing to understand the "immense methodological significance of Marx's analysis [of joint-stock companies]."*

If large joint-stock companies are for Marx and Engels an inevitable growth of capitalism, one could argue that as a necessary stage in capitalism's complete development, they are a step toward socialism. This is true in a sense, but it does not follow that stock companies are a "hidden transition," a dialectical transformation of capitalism into socialism. This transformation, as Marx says, stems from the maturation of the productive forces of capitalism.[53] It does not, one could add, stem from the transmutation of capitalist relations into capitalist relations of a higher order. Indeed, Marx's socialism is to be inaugurated by the producers, not by capitalism. Joint-stock companies, nonetheless, do display the intensifying conflict between social production and private appropriation, but this is a contradiction which is not limited to joint-stock companies. Rather, they are just one aspect of the general tendency of capitalist development —namely, the increasing concentration of capital in the hands of a few capitalists. After discussing this and the increasingly cooperative and social character of labor, Marx writes: "In both these ways, capitalist production eliminates private property and private labor, even though as yet in antagonistic forms."[54]

Why does this passage suggest that capitalism eliminates private property? Capitalism, of course, truncates production on the basis of individual property; this was Marx's first "negation." As the scale of production swells, capitalist property becomes even less individual. The concentrations of means of production

---

Capital 3: 437; Shlomo Avineri, *The Social and Political Thought of Karl Marx*, pp. 178–79n. This is characteristic of Avineri, who, like Lichtheim and others of his kidney, is abusive toward Lenin and at unbecoming pains to assert his own credentials, at the expense of those of Engels, as an interpreter of Marx.

appear not as individual property, but simply as "factors of social production." Despite the fact that the usufructuary of this is a dwindling class of capitalists, the increasingly centralized control of production does reflect its social character. Engels writes:

Partial recognition of the social character of the productive forces [is] forced upon the capitalists themselves. Taking over of the great institutions for production and communication, first by joint-stock companies, later on by trusts, then by the state. The bourgeoisie [is] demonstrated to be a superfluous class.*

But is this compatible with their earlier comments on the antagonistic stamp of this movement? Here, Engels is stating that the emergence of joint-stock companies and the rest is not just a continuation of the centralization of the means of production (due to the goad of capitalist competition) but also a move to accommodate the social nature of the productive forces. Such a notion, however, intimates that these developments might in fact succeed in attenuating the conflict between capitalism's productive forces and its relations of production.

This, I think, points to the historical limits of Marx's analysis. If the evolution of the competitive capitalism of the nineteenth century into the oligarchic, corporate capitalism of this century allowed the productive forces to be better accommodated (but this is a big issue!), then the epochal clash between these forces and their capitalist husk would be attenuated and, thus, the historical necessity and feasibility of socialism diminished. Marx may have presciently identified the tendencies of capitalist evolution, but he never thought that any development under the rule of capital would lessen the antagonism between the productive forces and the relations of production. And he never believed that anything less than truly cooperative relations between society's producers could satisfactorily and stably harness the productive forces fabricated by capitalism. However, were this

*Selected Works 3: 151; Capital 3: 120n. Marx writes in the Grundrisse that "as soon as [capital] begins to sense itself and become conscious of itself as a barrier to development, it seeks refuge in forms which, by restricting free competition, seem to make the rule of capital more perfect." Nonetheless, this heralds the dissolution of capitalism. See pp. 651–52 (Dietz ed., pp. 544–45).

shown to have happened, Marx's own theory of history could account for the failure of his prognostication by demonstrating that socialism was not necessary for the resolution of the disjunction between the productive forces and the relations of production in competitive capitalism.

Dialectics and the Proletariat

In the previous section, Avineri's exaggerated emphasis on the importance of joint-stock companies and cooperatives in Marx's thought was suggested to have been prompted by a faulty grasp of the nature of Marxian dialectics. Accordingly, I will first discuss the character of Marx's dialectical approach before briefly explicating the significance of the role of the revolutionary proletariat in his conception of the triumph of socialism.

The transition from capitalism to socialism would, following Avineri, seem essentially to be a performance of the historical dialectic—choreographed by a Marx who was never exorcised from the enchantment of Hegel's *List der Vernunft*. The intellectual relationship between Hegel and Marx is of course complex, and the voluminous scholarship on the subject testifies to its perennial fascination. It will not, therefore, be possible to do justice to it here, and this section contents itself with elucidating one simple and distinctive—but often obscured—aspect of Marxian dialectics: to wit, for Marx and Engels the dialectical method, if one may call it that, notwithstanding its other virtues, does not provide a mode of proof. Their obvious enjoyment of dialectical formulations and their satisfaction when even Hegel's idealistic recipes receive apparent empirical confirmation should not be taken to belie this. Marx and Engels were too loyal to the standards of science to think that dialectics itself provided explanations or justifications.

The fruitfulness of the dialectical approach results from the value, in Marx's view, of attempting to grasp reality as a process (both in the sense of flux and change and in the sense of development proper) whose component parts are not only intertwined but occasionally united as opposing trends within the same process or thing. To this end, dialectics demands a sensitivity to the antagonisms in things or, at least, in processes and relations, to their development and change, and to their interconnection within a framework larger than that of cause and effect (narrowly understood). In the afterword to the second edition of *Capital*, Marx affirmed the revolutionary consequences of such an approach in the social sciences.[55]

On the other hand, Marx also highlighted the importance of a dialectical presentation of the results of such an investigation. Although in *Capital* he refers to "coquetting" with the modes of expression peculiar to Hegel, his dialectical presentation has an importance which goes deeper than this. Precisely because the reality to be presented was in Marx's opinion dialectical, the method of presentation had to be suited to it. In the section on value in *Capital* this appears rather formalized, but the posthumous "Introduction" to the *Grundrisse* suggests that Marx's exposition of capitalist relations was intended to reflect in more subtle and profound ways the fundamental traits of the capitalist mode of production.[56]

Be this as it may, the propensities of capitalist development which Marx believed his *Capital* captured were neither guaranteed by his dialectical approach to the subject nor demonstrated because of the amenability of his analysis to dialectical presentation. This amenability, however, was a good sign: "Only after this work is done, can the actual movement be adequately described. If this is done successfully, if the life of the subject-matter is ideally reflected as in a mirror, then it may appear as if we had before us a mere a priori construction."[57] Why this post factum virtue of the analysis should be more than an aesthetic concern is not entirely certain. One presumes that Marx held the a-prioristic conviction that if (and only if) the real interconnections of a subject were grasped, then it would yield to such a rationalistic exposition.

All this is important in regard to the "negation of negation" passage from *Capital* with which Avineri toys. Although socialism may be represented as a dialectical overcoming of capitalism, it is not this which either effects or underwrites its arrival. Engels makes this point in defending Marx's procedure against Dühring's charge of "Hegelian word-juggling":

In characterizing the process as the negation of the negation, therefore, Marx does not dream of attempting to prove by this that the process was historically necessary. On the contrary: after he has proved from history that in fact the process has partially already occurred, and partially must occur in the future, he then also characterizes it as a process which develops in accordance with a definite dialectical law. That is all.[58]

The fact that neither the "negation of negation" nor any similar dialectical legerdemain is intended within historical materialism to verify (nor could it) the inevitability of socialism also implies that neither dialectical nor philosophical props to the proletariat's claim to be capitalism's gravedigger furnish its real (in Marx's view) scientific, historical justification. However, Marx and Engels, one must recall, were philosophical communists before they hammered out their materialist theory of history—let alone their sophisticated economic analysis. Thus, in 1844 for example, the proletariat was to be the emancipator of society because its suffering is universal, because it represents "a *total loss* of humanity . . . which can only redeem itself by a *total redemption of humanity*."[59]

Although remnants of this early, rather romantic attachment to the proletariat may be discerned throughout the writings of Marx and Engels, the analysis of *Capital* should have shown that in their mature works the revolt of the proletariat is firmly anchored in the material relations of production, and its sociohistorical office is determined by the conflict of the productive forces with their ownership relations. This is something which often fails to be appreciated by those who accent the more philosophical aspects of the proletariat's ascension—such as the Lukácsian Marxists, who identify the proletariat as at once the subject and object of history, as a class which (apparently) triumphs (owing to its unique perspective on society and history as "totality") simply by attaining self-consciousness. Such Hegelian-like themes are neither entirely alien to Marx's thought nor necessarily unprofitable, but they are not part of historical materialism: it was not for such reasons that Marx and Engels considered their adherence to the cause of the working class to be scientific.

In the first volume of *Capital*, Marx portrays the revolt of the working class as a result of the increasing misery of both employed and unemployed workers. The revolution of the proletariat is no deus ex machina introduced into Marx's theoretical perspective; it is a continuation of the historic class struggle between labor and capital which surges across the pages of capitalism's history. Marx saw all history as the record of wrangling between classes, of contention rooted in the material relations of these classes, and after his first trip to Paris as a young man, he was certain of the reality of working class rebellion. The actual history of the trade-union movement would seem both to document the existence of such a class struggle under capitalism and to have satisfied Marx's historical imperative that

the laborers must put their heads together, and, as a class, compel the passing of a law, an all-powerful social barrier that shall prevent the very workers from selling, by voluntary contract with capital, themselves and their families into slavery and death. In place of the pompous catalogue of the "inalienable rights of man" comes the modest Magna Charta of a legally limited working-day.[60]

But why should this economic revolt of the working class harden into social revolution? Marx's answer should already be apparent: as the contradictions inherent in capitalist production strengthen during its historical career so does the antagonism between classes. The *Communist Manifesto*, of course, proclaims that capitalist society divides more and more into two great classes, and this polarization would surely seem to sharpen the conflict. Even though Marx's later view appears to countenance an increasing intermediary class,[61] he undoubtedly continued to see the capitalist class itself as a dwindling group whose interests are ever more clearly antagonistic to that of the bulk of the population. This is because capitalist production does not admit of a solution to the contradictions which rack it—within the framework of its relations of production. Its very nature implies that it is production for surplus-value, not human use; in addition, as has been seen, the means which it employs to accomplish this begin to subvert its capacity to carry on production at all. The capitalist class is indicted by its inability to manage the productive forces which it has called into existence, and its historical justification visibly falls away. "History is the judge—its executioner, the proletarian."[62]

Since the capitalist system cannot resolve its own contradictions and the capitalist class has no interest in altering it, to achieve economic emancipation the working class is required to conquer political power itself and reshape the mode of production.[63] This—in whatever manner it is accomplished by the class—means revolution. Marx allowed that the proletariat could in some circumstances take power peacefully,[64] and the *Manifesto* envisions the proletariat originally making only "economically insufficient and untenable" inroads on the old order.* But Marx held, nonetheless, that socialist relations of production cannot gradually supersede capitalist relations. The proletariat must more or less rapidly overthrow the capitalist relations and install a new mode of production. While Marx may have overlooked the historical feasibility of the "mixed" economy, he did not think that socialism would uproot capitalism by competing with it.

Marx affirms that the development of labor throughout history has been a source of poverty and destitution for workers and of wealth and culture for non-workers, but only capitalist society has fashioned the material conditions "which enable and compel the workers to lift this social curse."[65] Throughout history aggrieved slaves have resisted their external constraints, but only when production has developed sufficiently will the op-

---

Selected Works 1: 126. But these initial measures "in the course of the movement, outstrip themselves, necessitate further inroads upon the old social order, and are unavoidable as a means of entirely revolutionizing the mode of production." Marx later stated that the transitional measures envisioned by the *Communist Manifesto* "are and must be contradictory in themselves" (to Sorge, June 20, 1881).

pressed succeed in installing a regime conducive to the fullest burgeoning of human freedom.[66]

The working class in Marx's conviction is compelled by its material conditions of life to take the only real course of action available to it: revolution. But this should not be allowed to hide a certain tension in Marx's vision of the proletariat. Usually, this is held to reside in Marx's belief that a class which is so degraded and estranged will be able to usher in the new era.[67] Marx, though, was sensitive to the fact that socialist society must emerge from the womb of the old order and thus be stamped in every respect by its birth; but he also held that oppression breeds resistance into the workers, that their very exploitation under capitalism organizes, centralizes, and disciplines them, and that the experiences of class struggle will induce in them an awareness of the necessity of exercising their power to expropriate the capitalist class. "With the accumulation of capital, the class-struggle and, therefore the class-consciousness of the work-ingmen, develop."[68] In addition, despite the fragmentation and misery of the laborer under capitalism, another trend is apparent: "Modern Industry, by its very nature, therefore necessitates variation of labor, fluency of function, universal mobility of the laborer."[69]

Although one may find Marx's answer here a little too easy, there is another difficulty lurking: while the working class is organizing itself economically and politically, the very humdrum of its capitalist existence continually tends to narcotize it:

The advance of capitalist production develops a working-class, which by education, tradition, habit, looks upon the conditions of that mode of production as self-evident laws of Nature. The organization of the capitalist process of production, once fully developed, breaks down all resistance. . . . The dull compulsion of economic relations completes the subjection of the laborer to the capitalist.[70]

This "dull compulsion," rather than the distress of the working class, might well be the brake on the proletarian revolution. But while Marx occasionally railed against the political lethargy of the workers (at least in Britain), he undoubtedly held that the intensifying contradictions of capitalist production would disrupt the hypnotic rut of its relations of production. Crises, at least, would mobilize the workers.[71] If, however, the development of capitalist production relations, as suggested in the last section, were to be such that they could satisfactorily harness society's productive forces and thus minimize social bouleversement, then this "dull compulsion" might successfully benumb the working class's move to attain socialistic relations.

In any event, while earlier classes (slaves and serfs, for example) were also led to rebel, in Marx's opinion, by their material conditions, in the case of the proletariat these conditions underwrite its ultimate victory. Only the proletariat can intervene to redress the conflict between the productive forces and their relations of production, because it is the only class or party (1) which is motivated to implement the solution (namely, social control of production) that will provide economic stability, and (2) which is in a position to carry out such a resolution. In the absence of this, the productive forces will continue to push for more compatible relations of production—the socioeconomic consequences of which have already been examined. Here, then, lies the historical inevitability of the dictatorship of the proletariat leading to a classless society, the grasping of which Marx thought was among his significant discoveries.[72]

CHAPTER FOUR

The Long March to Capitalism

THE OVERRIDING concern of Marx's theoretical career was the study of the capitalist mode of production, the laws of its development and evolution. The observations of Marx and Engels on pre-capitalist society, on the other hand, rest on far less research and were never molded into a systematic analysis. For modes of production other than capitalism, Engels admitted, political economy in its widest sense "has still to be brought into being."[1]

This reflects, in part, the priority which they assigned to understanding the present rather than a lack of historical perspective or curiosity—for they were well read and knowledgeable, especially for their time, about much of world history. Generally speaking, Marx approached earlier social formations from the vantage point of capitalism, and was chiefly concerned to contrast capitalism's defining traits with those of previous forms. Marx also examined those bygone economic types to locate the manner in which capitalism's particular elements were born. This demonstration of capitalism's historical specificity implied for Marx the other half of its temporal finitude: if capitalism is a system which has not always existed, then there is no reason to think it will last forever.

Despite the risk of disproportionately emphasizing Marx's

work on pre-capitalist economic formations, this avenue of his thought must be explored—less for its intrinsic significance, perhaps, than for what it divulges about the general intellectual terrain of Marx's materialist conception of history. The following discussion often raises more problems than it solves for particular historical opinions held by Marx; indeed, the deficiency of his analyses of earlier modes of production is striking in view of the boldness of the "Preface" and of the claims advanced on behalf of his theory of history. Our comprehension of this theory, however, should be enhanced by delimiting its answers and delineating its areas of ambiguity. An investigation of Marx's theoretical perspective requires that the dialectic of productive forces and relations of production be traced through the panorama of his historical reflections. Although Marx's thinking is occasionally fleshed out, I do not intend to present a refurbished, improved "Marxist" account of the various historical issues which shall be touched upon. Such a task would presuppose, among other things, a firm grasp of Marx's theory of history, but the elucidation of that theory can only be accomplished by attending, more narrowly, to the views to which Marx specifically commits himself.

Primitive Communism and the Emergence of Class Society

It is well known that Marx considered human society prior to the beginnings of civilization as being a primeval species of communism. Although Marx interpreted pre-history as conforming to his materialist theory and although he and Engels became increasingly interested in historical anthropology, Marx himself never fully developed a discussion of this early communalism. Engels did attempt this, and there are sufficient indications of Marx's own attitudes to enable his conception of primitive communism to be presented in terms of the dialectic between productive forces and relations of production which has been probed so far. I shall first explicate Marx's portrait of early society as this is presented in his most sustained account of pre-history (in the *Grundrisse*), indicating how this picture was modified late in Marx's life by his enthusiastic study of Lewis Henry Morgan, the American anthropologist.[2] I shall then explore the productive dynamics which in Marx's view lead to class society.

Man, according to the *Grundrisse*, was originally migratory, and settled down at a later time. The earth in its virgin state "supplies man with necessaries or the means of subsistence ready to hand."[3] He gathers, hunts, fishes, and somewhat later begins to graze animals and till the soil. The tribal community appears not as the consequence but as the precondition of the appropriation and use of both the earth and the objective conditions of life. Men exist in a "naive" relation to the earth and regard themselves as its communal proprietors; in this sense, the community is the prerequisite of production. In such a society, the group itself appears as the basis of production, and its simple, material reproduction appears as its ultimate purpose.[4] In terms of a pet metaphor of Marx, early man had "not yet severed the umbilical cord that unites him with his fellowmen in a primitive tribal community."[5]

"Directly associated" labor developed spontaneously and originally characterized the early history of all now civilized races.[6] This fundamental relationship can realize itself in various ways, three basic types of which are exhibited by Marx in the *Grundrisse*. The first of these is the Asiatic type; there, the all-embracing primitive unity stands above the community and is embodied in the person of a despot. Of the various modifications of the early community, this form survives longest. The second form, the ancient classical one, is based not on the land (united with craft manufacture) but on the city as the center of a rural population. The community is organized by kinship along military lines. Private property appears to exist along with common land, although membership in the community is still the precondition for this private appropriation. The third form is the Germanic one, in which the community is an association, not a union; unlike the second (ancient classical) model, property is not regulated through the community. Rather, the community exists only in the relations between individual landowners (for example, in their communal assembly). The individual home, the household, is the economic unit.

It bears stressing that these are all types of primitive communism, of the relationship of "communal tribal members to the tribal land." [7] At the same time these secondary communal forms are modes of evolution out of the primordial stage: "From the different forms of primitive common property, different forms of its dissolution have been developed." [8] Marx goes on to suggest that the "various original types of Roman and Teutonic" property are traceable to different forms still observable in India, and there is no doubt that Marx—in the 1850's and 1860's—allowed for divergent routes out of the most aboriginal communism. [9]

Although Marx does not provide a very full or graphic account of these disparate communal forms, he does affirm his materialist program: "In the last instance the community and the property resting upon it can be reduced to a specific stage in the development of the forces of production of the laboring subjects—to which correspond specific relations of these subjects with each other and with nature." [10] This does not say, however, that the three communal types are not successive responses to one unilinear growth of the productive forces of primitive society, but Marx does believe that the productive forces which are available to a community at this early stage are largely dependent upon natural circumstance. This suggests that the forms of primitive community result from different, but contemporaneous, sets of productive forces: "Different communities find different means of production, and different means of subsistence in their natural environment. Hence, their modes of production, and of living, and their products are different." [11]

If anything, this linking of the form of primitive society with the level of available productive forces was later strengthened, in the eyes of Marx and Engels, by Lewis Henry Morgan's research. What is novel there is the discernment of a uniform logic of development in man's early history (for example, the successive stages of savagery and barbarism), and this is a clear theme in Marx—after his discovery of Morgan:

The archaic or primary formations of our earth consist themselves of a series of layers of different age, superimposed upon one another. Similarly, the archaic structures of society reveal a series of different social types corresponding to progressive epochs.[12]

And again:

Primitive communities are not all cut to a single pattern. On the contrary, taken together they form a series of social groupings, differing both in type and in age, and marking successive stages of development.[13]

Particularly relevant is Morgan's explicit assimilation of Germanic gens society to the Greco-Roman tribal community; thus, these are no longer taken to be disjunctive paths out of primitive communism. The difference which Marx originally postulated between them would be explained, in the light of Engels' and Marx's post-Morgan writings, as a result of anachronistically comparing societies at dissimilar stages.

   Marx's post-Morgan view is, bluntly, more unilinear. It can, of course, account for a variety of socio-historical divergences, but in the last analysis history progresses along a singular evolutionary impulse: no longer is there a hint of truly alternative trails to civilization. Saliently, the characteristics which the *Grundrisse* ascribes to the Germanic formation designate what Marx was to identify later as the old Germanic peasant community (the Mark) or its Russian cousin, the village commune. These forms represent the highest (or youngest) of society's archaic configurations, in which the extended ties of consanguinity have already been replaced by more nearly nuclear families. Ownership of land still resides in the community, but cultivation and appropriation of the fruits of labor are individual.[14] Although their existing instances are exceptional survivals, Marx (in 1881) locates them near the end of a continuum already traversed by ancient Greece and Rome. These communities are, Marx observes, "at the same time a transitional phase to the secondary formation, i.e., transition from society based on common property to society based on private property. The secondary formation comprises, as you must understand, the series of societies based on slavery and serfdom."[15] Antiquity always supplied Marx's model of the transition to class society and civilization, and slavery clearly plays a key role in this story; by contrast, neither slavery nor wealth differentials had yet intruded into the already mature village commune.

The emergence of slavery is a prominent motif in Marx's commentaries on the rise of civilization: slavery is engendered by and, in turn, disrupts the previously egalitarian community. Originally, he and Engels appear to have seen slavery as an extension of the servitude of the patriarchal family, but years later, following Morgan, Marx reversed this.[16] Generally, though, there is a basic continuity in the comments of Marx and Engels (from different periods) on slavery and on the unfolding of classical civilization, which always constituted their main example of the beginnings of class society. Their post-Morgan view differs only in that this particular historical pattern becomes, in essence, the sole paradigm of the demise of the pre-class epoch: any community evolving internally toward civilization would develop in a similar fashion. In fact, it is reasonable to suppose that Marx and Engels liked Morgan's work in the first place largely because his conception of the genesis of civilization agreed with theirs. Thus, the various writings of Marx and Engels can be pooled, with little distortion, to present one fairly consistent picture of the dynamics which induce the birth of civilization.

They identify two fundamental factors that account for the occurrence of slavery. The first is the warlike inclination of the tribes (for war is the source of slaves). With settled peoples, the only barrier to the enjoyment of the natural conditions of production—of the land—is some other community; thus, war is

one of the community's earliest tasks.[17] Tribalism leads to slavery not just because of incessant conflicts but because of the
nature of primal proprietorship: sharing through a community
the possession of the earth as given. But a conquered individual
is tribeless, and a vanquished tribe is propertyless; as such they
become merely "part of the *inorganic conditions* of the conquering
tribe's reproduction, which that community regards as its
own."[18] Thus the nature of the tribal relations of production
allows naturally for the introduction of slavery. The subjugated
individuals can only appear as material to be appropriated by
the community. Slavery is a secondary but "necessary and logical
result of property founded upon the community and upon labor
in the community."[19]

This argues only that primitive production relations are capable of accommodating slavery; the actual introduction of slavery
is shown, secondly, to depend on the level of material production. As Engels observes, slaves were useless to barbarians at the
lower stage of evolution because human labor was unable to
produce a noticeable surplus above subsistence.[20] However, this
changed with the development of cattle breeding, weaving, and
metalworking: surplus-producing labor-power then came into
demand. Engels stresses the significance of herding and traces a
key advance in productivity to the first great social division of
labor: the separation of pastoral tribes from the mass of barbarians. Human labor-power thus becomes more efficient, and the
gain in productivity spurred by this division of labor brings slavery in its wake.[21] Originally, the community possesses its slaves in
common, further binding the group together.[22] The crucial development, though, is the emergence of private property in
slaves, and this is fostered by the spread of exchange made possible by progress in material production.

The trade which begins between primitive communities produces by reaction the internal exchange of products, encourag-
ing barter between individuals and thus nascent private property.[23] Private ownership of certain possessions and instruments

of production develops early; it and corresponding economic differentiation are given another boost by the second great division of labor (handicrafts from agriculture), which in turn makes slavery even more consequential. The evolvement of private property is quickened by the second division of labor, the increased exchange of surplus products, and the introduction of money. Intimately associated with the emergence of private property is the rise of patriarchy. Tribal kinship ties are the mainstay of the primitive community and are closely connected with communal property. The introduction of father rule and thus monogamy inclines the community—under pressure from the developing productive forces—toward production by family units, thus opening the door wider to private ownership relations.

Eventually, wealth in the form of land comes into private possession. While earlier Engels suggests that communal ownership was overthrown because it was a fetter on continued agricultural development,[24] in *The Origin* it is subverted by individuals eager to own privately the land which they possess.[25] These two views are not incompatible, but the second does intimate that the ownership relations of production are brought into correspondence with already existing work relations based on private familial production. This appears, in Marx's account, to be the developmental tendency of the Russian village commune, where private work relations reside within the husk of communal ownership. Free individual ownership arises only with the dissolution of organic society.[26] When the members of the community have acquired their separate existence as private proprietors, writes Marx, the conditions already exist which allow them to lose their property.[27] Mortgages and usury combine with individual exchange, money wealth, and commercial trade to shred the old gentile equality.

The emergence of class society, thus, actually consists of two distinct, although perhaps chronologically overlapping, moments. The first of these is the appearance of private property in

land; thus Marx speaks of "free self-managing peasant proprietorship" prevailing during the best periods of classical antiquity,
after the dissolution of the original community and prior to the
advent of a full-fledged slave mode of production.[28] While originally communal production and consequently the egalitarian
appropriation of the products of labor was made necessary by
the very low level of productive development, as the productive
forces grow they are more suitably handled by individual family
units, and tend to be consolidated in private ownership relations.
Private property comes as a response to the growing productive
capacity of society, but it also admits inegalitarian possession of
wealth and of the productive forces. Hence, its incidence within
the gens community is not a stable development but carries
within it the seeds of the community's destruction; this is the
second moment in the evolution of class society.

Thus Marx notes, in apparent opposition to Morgan, that already at the time of Theseus in Greece, "the chiefs of the gentes
etc., through wealth etc. had already reached a conflict of interest with the common people of the gentes, which is unavoidably
connected through private property in houses, lands, [and]
herds with the monogamous family."[29] The thinkers of antiquity
recognized that the growth of wealth meant the disintegration of
the community.[30] Changed economic conditions disrupted the
gentile social organization and encouraged the political restruc-
turing of society to correspond to the changed mode of production. Private ownership relations dissolved the old communal
production and burst their primitive political and social integument. In discussing this, Morgan describes the inability of the
gens to hold their members together in one place as a coherent
body. Marx notes this in his workbook and adds: "Aside from
locality: property difference[s] within the same gens had transformed the unity of their interests into antagonism of its members; in addition, besides land and cattle, money capital had become of decisive importance with the development of slavery!"[31]
As the gentile social structure crumbles, an aristocracy of wealth

is able to consolidate itself, and there is an enormous growth of slavery. With the previous political organization rent asunder, a new superstructure is raised on the basis of the slave mode of production: a state now rules a society cleaved by classes, a society divided into free men (rich and poor) and slaves.[32] Civilization has arrived.

The Natural Economies

> The system of production founded on private exchange [implies] . . . the historic dissolution of this naturally arisen [primitive] communism. However, a whole series of economic systems lies in turn between the modern world . . . and the social formations whose foundation is already formed by the dissolution of communal property.
>
> —*Grundrisse,* 882

Although Marx and his followers have been skeptical of categorizing economies as either "natural" or "money" economies, thereby obscuring what is truly definitive of capitalism, Marx himself observes that all modes of production prior to capitalism are "natural" in the sense that they are predominantly geared to the production of use-values—rather than exchange-values for a market.[33] These natural modes of production are alike in failing to encourage the rapid improvement of the productive forces; although their relations of production change and develop under pressure from the historically expanding productive forces, capitalism by contrast appears unique in actually requiring the continual advancement of those forces. Not surprisingly, in view of their low productive development, these economies are primarily oriented to the land, and it is agriculture that provides the bulk of their produce and the surplus by means of which their rulers live.

Mankind's progression through the Asiatic, the ancient slave, and the feudal modes of production constitutes the fundamental series of natural economies to which Marx refers above. They might be considered as ideal types comprising progressive epochs in man's history, to which particular social formations have more or less accurately corresponded.* This section undertakes to describe their prominent features and the logic of their development. Although Marx's materialist conception of history is illuminated by this exercise, it will be obvious that Marx does not adequately account for the nature and necessity of this evolution. That "economic history [was] still in its swaddling clothes" might be an extenuating consideration.[34] In any event, his theory, which trumpets the unity of man's historical development, does not in itself satisfactorily demonstrate the continuity and inexorability of that evolution, though Marx claims to lay the foundation for its scientific study.

Asia: Frozen on the Threshold of Civilization

The "Preface" lists the Asiatic mode of production as the first of society's progressive economic formations, and recent years have seen much discussion of it. For reasons peculiar to the trajectory of Marxist (or, more specifically, Soviet) historiography, much of the debate has sought only to show that Marx did not intend to subsume Asian society under either the ancient (slave) or feudal mode of production.[35] Since others have reported, more or less correctly, the course of Marx's reflections on Asia, for present purposes it will not be necessary to rehearse exhaustively all of Marx's comments on the Orient in order to elicit the most relevant points.[36]

Like Hegel, Marx perceived the dawn of civilization in the East; but while the first rays of civilization shone there, it was not until the sun moved west that it was able to rise above the horizon. Although Marx was greatly concerned with the details of Western capitalism's unwrapping of the mummified Orient, the original cause of the East's stagnancy did not appear very complex to him. He reports to Engels:

*Engels, for example, doubts if "feudalism ever correspond[ed] to its concept," but he would have wished to bestow more objectivity upon the concept than the term "ideal type" might be thought to suggest. Engels to Schmidt, March 12, 1895; to Kautsky, September 20, 1884.

The stationary character of this part of Asia—despite all the aimless movement on the political surface—is fully explained by two circumstances which supplement each other: (1) the public works were the business of the central government; (2) besides this the whole empire, not counting the few larger towns, was resolved into *villages*, each of which possessed a completely separate organization and formed a little world in itself.[37]

In the *Grundrisse*, it will be recalled, the Asiatic form is presented as the first historical modification within the primitive communism of man's primordial tribal existence. Here, the all-embracing unity which is the spontaneous, natural character of primeval social existence stands above the community itself. This unity appears as the real owner, the precondition of communality, thus enabling a despot to personify it and to appear as the father of the community, to whom its surplus product naturally and rightfully belongs.[38] This form of primitive community survives longest and most stubbornly because of the self-sustaining circle of production upon which it rests, and its tribal or common property, which is "in most cases created through a combination of manufacture and agriculture," provides the requisite foundation of Oriental despotism.[39]

The *Grundrisse*'s three types of primitive communism are also three modes of its dissolution. The Asiatic form, however, is at best only a partial dissolution of the early community. The general, slavish character of this society, along with its communality, implies that the individual's organic, umbilical ties to his community and to nature have not been severed. Thus, the timeless Asian village (abstracted from its subjection to despotic rule) comes to represent for Marx primitive communism itself, as seen by his assertion "that the Asian or Indian forms of property constitute the initial ones everywhere in Europe."[40] Marx does not mean that Europe passed through the Asiatic mode of production but that it developed from the primitive community, of which India offers "a sample chart of the most diverse forms."[41]

The Indian forms themselves, however, comprise only remnants, descended from primitive communism. Aside from its longevity in Asia, there is nothing particularly Oriental about this original communal property—an opinion which emerges clearly in the later writings of Marx and Engels. Thus Engels observes in an 1888 footnote to the *Manifesto* that the village communities have been found "to have been the primitive form of society everywhere from Ireland to India."[42] Similarly, the English translation of the first volume of *Capital*, supervised by Engels, at one point renders "das ursprünglich *orientalische* Gemeineigentum" as "the primitive form of ownership in common."[43]

The Eastern village is characterized not only by its communality but by its specific unity of small handicraft manufacture and agriculture, a label which Marx frequently repeats but rarely embroiders. *Capital* briefly sketches the unalterable social division of labor in an Indian village and credits its classic "simplicity" with providing the secret to the "unchangeableness" of Asiatic society.[44] The traditional organization of labor petrifies productive development, but Marx never explains the emergence of such relations except to hint that the caste system is not an unnatural occurrence.[45] Although he acknowledges the quality of Indian craftsmanship, the limited productive growth which goes occur in the village is successfully contained within customary ownership and work relations. But how can this community be the original form from which all others evolved and yet provide the basis for the static, unchanging nature of Asiatic society?[46]

To answer this, one must turn to that other circumstance which, according to Marx's letter to Engels, assures the stagnacy of Asiatic production. The public works to which he refers there are the large-scale irrigation projects, indispensible to agricultural production in the vast areas of the Orient and Africa. Such projects, given the primitive character of the productive forces, could only be maintained by a strong central government—the type of despotic regime characteristic of Asia.[47] This despotic state (and Marx at least occasionally acknowledges its extensive bureaucratic features)[48] would explain the stationary nature of Asiatic production: the continual drain of surplus from the already motionless village unity of domestic manufacture and diminutive agriculture would guarantee the community's productive inertia.

The Oriental towns, according to François Bernier, whose description Marx accepts, are little more than traveling camps, geared to the consumption of the agricultural surplus which flows to the despotic ruler.[49] The agricultural surplus also supports a "swarming non-agricultural population" in the cooperative production of enormous "works of magnificence or utility."[50] Since the bulk of the villages' surplus is consumed by the government for administration, defense, opulent living, and the construction of public works, the villagers themselves are left with neither the means nor an incentive for improving their productive forces. The development which does occur takes place within petrified work relations of production. The despotic government not only leaves these relations undisturbed but hermetically seals off the community from external contact.[51]

The urban development and commerce permitted by the centralization and accumulation of surplus is not an expression of internal commodity production but of the transformation of this surplus into commodities: the towns produce luxury goods for the autocrat.[52] This monopolization of wealth and the absence of competition militate against industrial innovation: neither the ruler nor the craftsman would seem to have an interest in increasing productivity.

Although *Capital* stresses that "one of the material bases of the power of the State over the small disconnected producing organisms in India, was the regulation of the water supply," this immediate economic explanation of despotism begins fading from Marx's writings rather quickly.[53] *Capital*'s description of an Indian village, for instance, mentions irrigation briefly but does not identify it as a function of the state, "into whose hands from time immemorial a certain quantity of these [surplus] products has found its way in the shape of rent in kind."* The state stands over the direct producers simultaneously as sovereign and landlord; only with the coming of British rule of India is private property with private landlords introduced. Prior to that, village land is possessed both in common and by individuals while rent and taxes combine to form one tribute flowing traditionally to the state as supreme lord.[54]

Marx leaves rather unclear the precise nature of Asian ownership relations, or what sort of control the state has over the productive forces, especially since he no longer assigns it a directly economic function. He does write that where the small peasants "form among themselves a more or less natural community, as they do in India . . . the surplus-labor for the nominal owner of the land can only be extorted from them by other than economic pressure, whatever the form assumed may be," but this is not elaborated.[55] Generally, in Marx's theory the existence of a state implies a class society (and hence the dissolution of primitive communism) over which its rule is necessary in order to hold the social fabric together. In Asia, however, the state represents not so much a ruling class, but one person: the despot is not simply the head of the state but appears as its raison d'être.[56]

The production relations of the Asiatic mode curtail any serious advancement of the productive forces; they correspond to those forces but are not forms of their development. Neither the progress of production nor the accrual of wealth (outside the state) is sufficient for differences of status to produce economic divisions disruptive of the village. In particular, the emergence of private property in land is thwarted. All the separate villages and their various members are equal in their general slavery to the despot; private slavery is unable to develop. The introduction of materially feasible productive forces may possibly be prevented by the relations of production, but the existing productive forces themselves are not fettered since they never mature

---

Capital 1: 357. Rent in kind is "quite adapted to furnishing the basis for stationary social conditions as we see, e.g., in Asia." *Capital* 3: 796; 1: 140–41.

enough to conflict with their primitive encasement. The Asiatic mode is not so much a case of the successful hampering of the productive forces by their relations as it is a paralysis of both aspects of production: its specific character stunts all material and social progress. Asia remains frozen on the threshold of civilization, outside the mainstream of history.

The Ancient Mode of Production

While the Asiatic mode of production has been the subject of some interest among Marxists, Marx's reflections on classical production have not been so blessed. That Marx assigned a definite mode of production to antiquity has never been doubted, and it has been assumed, perhaps a little too readily, that its make-up is transparent. Indeed, Marx's view of classical production appears definite and simple: he saw both Greek and Roman society as embodying a mode of production constituted by slave production. Direct forced labor, in his opinion, was the foundation of the ancient world, and the mass of its productive labor was performed by slaves. Nonetheless, Marx did not bequeath a clear analysis of the economic dynamics of the ancient world, of its necessary evolution, or of its connection with feudalism. This legacy is a much greater handicap to construing his theory of history than the insufficiency of his comments on either primitive communism or Oriental production.

Earlier, the momentum of classical gens society was reviewed, and an originally egalitarian, barbaric community was seen to give way under the pressure of society's increasing productive capacity. Private property is inaugurated, and then, almost simultaneously, small proprietors begin capitulating in the face of a spreading slave production, controlled by wealthy patricians. The triumph of large-scale slave production over petty agriculture lies behind Marx's hint in *Capital* that the secret history of the Roman republic "is the history of its landed property,"[57] a clue which had already been expanded upon in a letter to Engels: "A little time ago I went through Roman (ancient) history again up to the time of Augustus. The internal history resolves itself plainly into the struggle of small with large landed property, naturally specifically modified by slave relations."[58]

This is merely the continuation of the process which destroyed the gens and consolidated the ancient slave mode of production: the patricians, alleges Marx, squeezed dry the plebeians with usury and military service, replacing their small properties with a slave economy.[59] Although antiquity continued to bear the marks of its gentile birth, one must distinguish, following Marx, (1) the decline of the communal gens, with the accompanying establishment of private (usually small) property in land from (2) the time when slavery "seized upon production in earnest," and the ancient mode of production proper emerged.[60]

Slavery is perhaps the key factor in dissolving the original community and forms the basis of the ancient mode of production; only with its entrance, according to the *Anti-Dühring*, is significant productive progress accomplished by mankind—a qualitative advance beyond Asiatic production.[61] Slavery realizes the potential of the productive forces and ensures their further development—at the expense of the direct producers, to be sure. Marx saw the ancient mode of production as being grounded in large-scale landed property with the latifundium as its basic production unit. In addition, slaves performed household work and were employed industrially. Industry itself had a "landed-proprietary" character and was completely dependent upon agriculture.[62] While the slave system did produce for the city market, the latifundia preserved a natural economy in which both spheres of production were integrated.

Although the Roman world saw the spread of commerce, the aim of classical production remained primarily the production of use-values for the slave-owners. There was no real investment in production, and although bankruptcy did occur in antiquity, there were no crises as such.[63] Wealth was produced for private consumption: "the ancients never thought of transforming the surplus-product into capital."[64] The ruling class appears to have had little interest in expanding the productive forces under its aegis, and in fact these never developed beyond handicraft labor. The relations of production could not have accommodated the production for production's sake of bourgeois society, and in this regard the ancient mode of production is akin to Asiatic or feudal production.

Unfortunately, Marx never connected the ancient mode of production to the imperial expansion of Rome or clarified its relation to Roman commerce. (Possibly, Roman slave production required territorial extension both to gather fresh labor-power and to provide new land for colonization—since land ownership was the prerequisite of full Roman citizenship.)[65] As a result, Engels' story of the growing unprofitability of slave production in the later Roman empire—due to the impoverishment of the masses, the decay of cities, and the decline of trade—is insufficiently underpinned.[66] He accounts for the tendency of the latifundia to be parceled out among hereditary tenants bound to the land (the coloni), but an explanation fastening this to the impetus of Rome's economy and empire is not proffered.

That slave relations of production, beyond a certain point, erect barriers to the improvement of the productive forces was for Marx just as certain as their initially progressive character. In the first place, slavery of the nonpatriarchal type is wasteful of labor-power, of the slaves themselves: "the most effective economy is that which takes out of the human chattel in the shortest space of time the utmost amount of exertion it is capable of putting forth."[67] If the sources of slaves—basically, war and plunder—were to dry up, then society could hardly rely on slave relations to ensure continued material production (at the same level). In addition, the slaves themselves are reckless with the means of production: only the rudest and heaviest implements are compatible with slave labor.[68] Supervision time is great, and slave labor-power tends to be inflexible and to be employable only in conventional modes.[69] Finally, as a result of slavery, material production itself bore a stigma in antiquity.[70] Obviously, slave relations of production limit productive progress, but Marx never reveals with what ancient productive forces they clash.

Even though this omission raises problems in interpreting the emergence of feudal relations of production, it is compatible with Marx's apparent belief that, despite the disintegration (for whatever reasons) of the ancient mode of production, the productive forces which it harbored did not furnish the elements capable of being reorganized in higher relations. This is apparent upon examination of the double class struggle of antiquity: "freeman and slave, patrician and plebeian."[71] On the one hand, while the slaves were capable of fettering production and were no doubt motivated to do so—Marx writes that the antagonism between direct producer and the owner of the means of production is greatest under slavery—they did not embody an alternative to the ancient mode of production. Engels denies that slaves can emancipate themselves as a class; in antiquity only the manumission of individuals was possible.[72] On the other hand, the ruined plebeians, surviving like cancerous cells in the breast of antiquity, represented only the memory of a vanquished mode of production—petty landed proprietorship; they marked no historically viable alternative to continued slave production. Slave production, in fact, was the "passive pedestal" for the struggle of free rich and free poor.[73]

Despite the fact that the rabble had been divorced from the means of production and were potential proletarians, Roman conditions, as Marx often stressed, were premature for capitalist production.[74] He never particularized these remarks, but antiquity did enjoy widespread commerce and the (consequent) disintegration of traditional relations of production, resulting in concentrations of wealth, on the one hand, and "free" laborers (or potential laborers) on the other. The missing prerequisite would clearly have been, in Marx's opinion, a sufficient advancement of the productive forces. Without that, capitalist relations were unable to develop—despite the existence of commerce, money, and rudimentary commodity production.

Although a "revolutionary re-constitution of society at large" was not on the productive-force cards dealt to Rome, class struggle appears in Marx's view to have been responsible for sealing antiquity's fate. Indeed, the ancient world seems to be the prime referent of the *Manifesto*'s mention of class conflict ending "in the common ruin of the contending classes."[75] While Marx considered Spartacus to be the "most splendid fellow" of antiquity,[76] the slave struggle does not appear to be what Marx and Engels had in mind, and it would be tendentious to claim, as some of their Soviet followers have, that ancient slavery was destroyed by the joint revolutionary struggle of slaves and free peasants.[77] Rather, it was the patrician-plebeian conflict which ate away at the heart of Greece and Rome; Engels in fact states that the pauperized free citizens of Athens precipitated the downfall of the Athenian state.[78] This indicates all the more vigorously the absence of any serious discussion by Marx of the dynamics of the ancient mode of production: the class struggle which brought it down simply reversed the patrician victory which had originally consolidated this social formation.

The Development of Feudal Relations

For reasons not made entirely transparent by Marx, the Roman imperial structure decays, and the manorial slave production typical of the ancient mode proves uneconomical and obsolete. In an apparent anticipation of feudalism, the slave plantation gradually yields in favor of hereditary tenancies. Finally, the sagging empire is collapsed by the Germanic invasions. In line with the earlier remarks on class struggle, Engels asserts that the oppressed and extorted citizens of the Roman empire welcomed the barbarians as liberators.[79] In the process of ruling the extensive areas liberated from Roman dominion, however, the organs of the Germanic gens transmute into organs of state —although remnants of the gens can be observed in the peasant commune or Mark, which subsists surreptitiously under feudalism.[80]

The Middle Ages started from the country. From the outset,

feudal development "extends over a much wider territory, prepared by the Roman conquests and the spread of agriculture at first associated with them."[81] According to Engels, the Germanic invasions are followed by a period of peasant proprietorship. Serfdom insinuates itself, however, essentially as a response to the disorder that is enveloping society. Wars and feuds between nobles, the plundering of the Norse, as well as the covetousness of the lords and the church led the peasants to seek protectors; after a few generations, hereditary dependency relations were fairly common everywhere.[82] For convenience, I shall refer to this account of the emergence of serfdom as the "conjunctural" explanation. It receives support from Marx's assertion that the obligations of military service were the means by which "Charlemagne brought about the transformation of free German peasants into serfs and bondsmen" and from his description of the introduction of corvée labor in Roumania.[83]

However, Marx does intimate that dependent labor was important for the German tribes even before Charlemagne's conquests:

The Germanic barbarians, who lived in isolation on the land and for whom agriculture with bondsmen [mit Leibeignen] was the traditional production, could impose these conditions on the Roman provinces all the more easily as the concentration of landed property which had taken place there had already overthrown the earlier agricultural relations.[84]

Whereas in *The German Ideology* the invasions were an example of the "destruction of an old civilization by a barbarous people and the resulting formation of an entirely new organization of society," the *Grundrisse*, from which the above passage is drawn, makes a slight qualification: the Germanic conquests produce a synthesis of two modes of production, "in part."[85] Although admittedly equivocal, this may suggest not that a Roman-Germanic mixing failed to occur, but that the two modes of production were not, in fact, so dissimilar. The twilight of the Empire had brought a loss of productive forces. As Engels later put it: "conquered and conquerors were almost at the same stage of economic development and thus the economic basis of society remained the same as before."* This adds a little more continuity to the story of the burgeoning of seignorial relations: if the Germanic tribes had already developed relations of production comparable to those of the Greek or Roman gens at the threshold of the slave mode of production, had used enthralled labor-power, and had suffered wealth differentials among their families, then their conquest of spacious landed estates, either worked by slaves or already parceled out among coloni, would have been propitious for the eventual emergence of large landowners and a dependent peasantry. It also accords better with Engels' belief that the early Middle Ages saw innumerable degrees of serfdom and slavery than does the postulation of an intermediary stage of universal peasant proprietorship.[86]

Although both Marx and Engels do appeal to the "conjunctural" factors of war, pillage, and the general insecurity of the Middle Ages, these impulses cannot explain—within their theory—the consolidation of feudal production. If anything, the violent social conditions of the Dark Ages would have to be explained by the existing relations of production. Thus, Marx's thesis requires it to be the case not only that (1) Germanic gens society reacted noncommunally to its new productive force environment, and that (2) manorial production accommodated the available productive forces better than an independent peasantry (or a slave system), but that (3) these (feudal) relations of production were brought about because of (2).

Marx and Engels do indeed underscore the dependence of feudal property on the existing productive forces. After specif-

---

*Selected Works 3: 326, 313–14. This accounts for the commutation of slaves to coloni, but it damages a traditional Marxist thesis that both the introduction of the latter and the later establishment of serfdom were due to the inefficacy of the previous relations in accommodating new, emergent productive forces. See Stalin, *Dialectical and Historical Materialism*, p. 36, and Ernst Hoffmann, "Social Economic Formations and Historical Science," p. 275. Although the feudal mode of production was to push society's productive capacity well beyond the level of antiquity, the transition to it appears to be preceded not only by the disintegration of the ancient mode of production but by a retrogression of the productive forces.

ically discussing their low level of development in the period of the conquest, they continue: "From these conditions and the mode of organization of the conquest determined by them, feudal property developed."[87] Since Engels later stressed that servitude in the Middle Ages was not simply based on the fact of conquest, the manner of organizing the subjugated land would seem to depend essentially on the agricultural productive forces.[88] In this regard, *The German Ideology* observes that "the form of community adopted by the settling conquerors must correspond to the stage of development of the productive forces they find in existence; or, if this is not the case from the start, it must change according to the productive forces."[89] These productive forces both require serf relations and ensure that they are established.

For Marx dependent labor, tied to the soil, constitutes the material basis of the medieval world, and generally Marxists have taken serfdom and demesne farming as its defining production relation.[90] Earlier, the fundamental nature of feudal relations of production was described: the peasant possesses—but does not own (privately)—the means of production with which he is both required to perform surplus labor for his lord and allowed to work on his own behalf. The nature of feudal rent (labor services, payment in kind, or money) varies, but the surplus produced for the peasant's superior is obvious and undeniable. The feudal system rests on the back of a subject peasantry. The personal dependence which marks feudal relations of production is generalized throughout society: one "find[s] everyone dependent, serfs and lords, vassals and suzerains, laymen and clergy."[91] The medieval world, for Marx, was essentially a product of serfdom, and he stresses the explanatory primacy of its economic structure—rather than its political, military, or religious patterns. "Feudalism itself had entirely empirical relations as its basis. . . . [F]eudalism is the political form of the medieval relations of production and commerce."*

***The German Ideology*, pp. 190, 364. See *The Revolutions of 1848*, p. 249: "Big landed property was in reality the basis of the medieval, *feudal society*." Engels

Within the feudal world, structured by this mode of production, craft labor could emerge only through the framework of the guild: on the one hand, only guild ownership relations could ensure the survival and development of the productive forces involved; on the other hand, the very mechanics of disposing labor-power and transmitting craft skill would have inclined the work relations toward the hierarchy of master-journeyman-apprentice. "Guild industry, in its heyday, found in the guild organization all the fullness of freedom it required, i.e., the relations of production corresponding to it."[92]

Marx apparently thought that these relations within the city imitated the feudal organization of the land, but the rise of the medieval town itself within a seignorial economy is not really explained by him. No doubt it was initially facilitated by the structure of manorial production (with the parceling of political sovereignty) as well as by increased agricultural productivity, and Marx does claim that serfs fleeing manorial persecution were responsible for swelling the urban population.[93] In some fashion, though, farm and guild do form one economic system, and this is a response to the existing productive forces, to the restricted material conditions of production.[94]

In what sense, then, is the ancient mode of production a necessary step toward this economic formation? Despite its internal decay and retrogression, the Roman empire did prepare the productive forces, in particular the landed estates, which were to provide the basis of feudal relations of production. One might suppose that in colonizing Gaul and Germania, Rome overextended the ancient mode of production by imposing latifundium-farming on a large area whose productive forces were not adequate for slave production (because, for example, of colder climate, sparser population). When for internal reasons these relations could no longer be artificially sustained, and as the supply of slaves diminished, the current was toward replacing plantation production with proto-feudal

thought it transparent that in feudalism "the form of state evolves from the form of economy." Engels to Mehring, September 28, 1892.

relations.[95] In addition, the continual contact of the slave mode
with the barbaric Germans would have raised the Germans' productive (and, obviously, military) capacity. But again what is
lacking is an explanation of the nature and cause of this expan-
sionism, which fashioned the productive forces to be appropriated by the Germans and woven into feudalism, in terms of the
tension between the productive forces and the relations of production within the ancient mode. Further, there is no conclusive
showing that *only* slave production can pave the path for feudalism.* It is certain, though, that the emergence of feudalism from
the synthesis of slave and barbaric modes of production, while
it may be viewed as an adaptation to the existing productive
forces, does attenuate the explosiveness of the "Preface" model
of socio-historical development.

The Transition from Feudalism to Capitalism

Even though Marx describes the preconditions of capitalist
production and some of the factors responsible for introducing
and consolidating capitalism, he does not provide a theory of the
transition from feudalism to capitalism—at least, not in the sense
in which he tendered a theory underwriting the arrival of socialism. He did sketch the appearance of capitalist production relations in England and discussed the genesis of its necessary elements, but the story related by *Capital* and the hints dropped
elsewhere must be distinguished from a theory explaining *why*
in general feudalism yields to the capitalist mode of production.
Although it shall be necessary to locate a few of the methodological peculiarities of the account which Marx proffers, this section
is directed neither toward recounting this entire historical narrative nor toward measuring it against the record of history
itself. Rather, the aim here is to illuminate those aspects of
Marx's presentation which reveal something of the character
of the dynamic of productive forces and relations of production

*This issue—unbroached by Marx—is complicated by his apparent acknowl-
edgment of the existence of non-European feudalism. See *Capital* 1: 718n and
Engels, *Anti-Dühring*, p. 201.

which Marx envisioned as underlying this socio-historical transformation.

It should be emphasized at the beginning that Marx's claim that the productive forces determine the relations of production is not embarrassed by his belief that the productive forces distinctive to capitalism emerge only after the general establishment of capitalist ownership relations. The determination thesis requires only that the installation of capitalist relations be a response to the existing level of the productive forces,[96] and indeed Marx and Engels explicitly endorse this position:

We see then: the means of production and of exchange, on whose foundation the bourgeoisie built itself up, were generated in feudal society. At a certain stage in [their] development . . . the feudal relations of property became no longer compatible with the already developed productive forces; they became so many fetters. They had to be burst asunder; they were burst asunder.[97]

Although they were to elaborate and elucidate this blunt passage from the *Communist Manifesto*, it continued to furnish the kernel of their perspective.

Their clarification of one aspect of this early statement is evident in a short but significant paragraph in *Capital*: "The economic structure of capitalistic society has grown out of [ist hervongegangen aus] the economic structure of feudal society. The dissolution of the latter set free the elements of the former."[98] This passage suggests two distinguishable steps: first, the dissolution of the feudal economic structure, and second, the combination of the freed elements into capitalist relations of production. About the first step, as shall be seen, Marx does not say enough: he takes it for granted in his account of history's preparation of the elements necessary for capitalist production. He argues that wherever capitalism appears (its era dates from the sixteenth century) "the abolition of serfdom has been long effected, and the highest development of the middle ages, the existence of sovereign towns, has been long on the wane."[99]

Feudalism decays prior to the commencement of capitalism. This permits Marx to trace the genealogy of the factors which

are brought together in capitalist relations of production without revealing the interior dynamics of the feudal mode of production itself. One should not suppose, however, as Etienne
Balibar does, that this implies that Marx viewed the emergence
of capitalism as independent of its feudal forebear. In fact,
Balibar perceives a "diversity of historical roads," a "plurality of
processes," leading to the establishment of capitalism, and the
context indicates that he has in mind the possibility of capitalism
arising from alternative, non-feudal modes of production.[100]
This raises an interesting issue, although two aspects of it are
fused.

Marx, in one sense, clearly allows for different routes to
capitalism. Although he later speaks of having described "the
path by which, in Western Europe, the capitalist order of
economy emerged from the womb of the feudal order of
economy,"[101] in fact Marx really only traces the itinerary which
England followed, and he states that the transition from
feudalism to capitalism "in different countries, assumes different
aspects, and runs through its various phrases in different orders
of succession, and at different periods."[102] On the other hand,
the fact of capitalism's different national evolutions does not
imply that they result from fundamentally different historic-
economic impulses, or that capitalism may sprout from ground
other than the remains of feudalism. Socialism, Marx thought,
will be attained by different peoples in their own fashion, but
this weakens neither the necessity of its arrival nor the basic discrepancy between productive forces and relations of production
which motivates its emergence. Similarly, capitalist relations
come to pass in each location via distinctive historical occur-
rences, but this alone does not attenuate the necessity of the
transition from feudalism to capitalism. To paraphrase Marx,
the general and necessary tendencies must be distinguished
from their forms of manifestation.

This still leaves unanswered the question of whether Marx believed that capitalism could emerge from a non-feudal social

formation. When questioned about the inevitability of capitalism in Russia, Marx characteristically denied propounding "any historico-philosophic theory of the *marche generále* imposed by fate upon every people," but this oft-quoted remark reveals less of an anti-determinismistic view than generally thought.* Marx discerned a logical and necessary pattern of development from Western feudalism through capitalism to socialism, but a higher economic form may influence a lower one, resulting in pre-feudal societies advancing directly into capitalism or pre-capitalist ones into socialism. Nowhere, however, does Marx suggest that capitalism could emerge internally and independently within a non-feudal society.

The decline of feudalism and the release of the productive forces which have nourished within it are prerequisites of capitalism's world debut. The manorial system, based on serfdom, constitutes the basis of medieval production, and frequently Marx emphasizes its peasant basis of small property and limited technique, Kleinbauernwirtschaft.[103] The feudal organization of agriculture was matched in the towns by the craft labor of artisans, organized in a guild hierarchy. However, this dual petty production, grounded in small-scale work relations, "flourishes, it lets loose its whole energy . . . only where the laborer is the private owner of his own means of labor set in action by himself: the peasant of the land which he cultivates, the artisan of the tool which he handles as a virtuoso."[104]

Since Marx wrote that in the last analysis the transition to capitalism is the transformation of one form of private property into another form of private property, "of the pigmy property of

---

*Letter to the Editor of *Notes on the Fatherland*, November 1877. For example, see D. R. Gandy's "Karl Marx's Philosophy of History: A New Interpretation." Gandy's new interpretation is simply that Marx's philosophy of history does not say that every nation on earth necessarily traverses the same four or five stages. Gandy's whole project suffers from his failure to understand that Marx could consistently believe in a necessary, productive-force-determined evolution of history without holding that every social group is preordained to follow the same course—uninfluenced by other societies at higher or lower stages of advancement. See above, pp. 79–81.

the many into the huge property of the few,"[105] the emancipation of this latent private property from its feudal encumbrance, which paves the ground for capitalism, must be explored.

In agriculture, the material reproduction of the peasant population requires no assistance from the lords they support; since the serfs are already in possession of their means of livelihood, the possibility of private peasant proprietorship lies dormant at the heart of the feudal system. The struggle of serfs and lords is endemic to feudal production, and Engels acknowledges "the silent work of the oppressed classes [which] undermined the feudal system throughout Western Europe and created conditions in which ever less room was left for the feudal lord."[106] The enforced labor of the serf is generally fixed, but his productivity on his own land is not: thus "the possibility is here presented for definite economic development."[107] It is reasonable to suppose, then, that the enlargement of agricultural productivity would induce the peasant to try to consolidate his rights to the product of his labor and his rights over the means of production in his possession. This interest is further whetted as labor rent—that is, cultivation by the serf of the lord's own land— yields to rent in kind and money rent, thus strengthening the grip of private property on the peasant. Money rent—although initially a type of feudal rent—is its "dissolving form."[108] With its development the personal relations of mastery and servitude are replaced by purely economic relations, and distinctively feudal production ceases.

The pressure of the subordinated peasantry alone, however, would not suffice to account for the demise of manorial production, since the resistance of the agricultural population to the demands of the nobility is the leitmotif of medieval history. Thus, to explain the decline of serfdom, some change in the relative position of the lord must occur, so that his advantage lies in commuting the feudal burdens on the peasantry (rather than simply in enforcing them more ruthlessly). But in the absence of a discussion by Marx of the dynamics of feudal production or of the intercourse of hinds and suzerains with the town, no definite explanation can be advanced on his behalf.

Regardless of how Marx saw the loosening of seignorial bonds in the country, the dissolving of these relations is only rendered possible by the development of the productive forces.[109] Private property in land not only constitutes the ownership relations which are appropriate (at this production stage) to the already existing small-scale, agricultural work relations; in addition, it "is as necessary for full development of this mode of production as ownership of tools is for free development of handicraft production."[110] This type of production encourages the advance of the productive forces and provides a basis for simple commodity production and exchange. Although production is by no means geared primarily for exchange, the division of labor between town and country, and within both, requires it to a certain extent.

Developments in the medieval town are dissimilar, however. Although the opening paragraphs of the *Communist Manifesto* refer to the struggle of "guild-master and journeyman," no analogous liberation of the small producer from the guild occurs. This is because guild production itself represents in part a disruption of feudal production relations: the movable property and craft labor which comprise the conditions of the existence of the urban dwellers and corporations are separated from their feudal ties only to be asserted against feudal landed property in a feudal form.[111] The communes of the burghers did constitute commercial islands within the feudal countryside and were a step in the development of the bourgeoisie,[112] but urban production remains within its quasi-feudal shell until it is replaced by capitalist production. "Though urban crafts are based substantially on exchange and the creation of exchange-values, the main object of production is not *enrichment* or *exchange-value as exchange-value*, but the *subsistence of man as an artisan, as a master-craftsman*, and consequently use-value."[113]

While Marx does not fully explicate the dynamics of town and country, the gradually evolving economic preponderance of the town—in particular, the productive heights reached by urban craft labor—is of signal importance. The division of labor between guilds (although not within them) develops quite naturally; it reflects the level of the productive forces as they exist within feudal society and promotes their development.[114] Handicraft work grows in quality and efficiency as the labor-skills cultivated by the guilds increase and their tools become more precise. The work and ownership relations of production are conducive to individual craftsmanship and the gradual improvement of the productive forces. Eventually, however, the relations of production which protected and supported this productive growth begin to hamper it. Marx writes: "Urban labor itself had created the means of production, for which guilds became as great an embarrassment as were the old relations of landed property in an improved agriculture, which was in turn partly the consequence of the greater sale of agricultural products to the cities, etc."[115]

Although petty production in agriculture wriggles free from its feudal bindings and boosts the productive forces, the work relations associated with it soon fail, as do the guild relations of the town, to realize the full potential of the productive forces which they harbor. They exclude concentration of the means of production, cooperation, and division of labor within the production process—in a word, they prohibit the larger, technical production which the level of the productive forces makes possible.[116] The guilds in fact specifically restrained the master from becoming a capitalist by limiting both his capital and the number of men which he might hire.[117] Capitalist (ownership) relations of production are the necessary condition for transforming the labor process into a social process.[118]

With the dissolving of feudal production relations, and the spreading of private property and the monetary relations associated with it, the extension of exchange and commerce unleash the forces which precipitate primitive accumulation. At a certain stage in its development, the petty production which precedes capitalism "brings forth the material agencies for its own dissolution. From that moment new forces and new passions spring up in the bosom of society."[119] These currents underlie the "primitive [ursprünglich] accumulation" of the elements necessary for capitalism to begin: a population of free laborers, stripped of both feudal encumbrances on their labor-power and means of production sufficient for their independent subsistence, and monetary accumulations capable of being converted into the means necessary for industrial production. The final section of *Capital* discusses the expropriation of England's agricultural population and describes the despicable manner by which capital came into the world, "dripping from head to foot, from every pore, with blood and dirt."[120] The accumulation of capital is fed primarily by the colonial system, commercial wars, over-taxation, and protectionism, which in turn reveal a record of looting, enslavement, oppression, and greed. These are merely the forcible means which, along with the expulsion of the peasantry from the land, serve "to hasten, hothouse fashion, the process of transformation of the feudal mode of production into the capitalist mode, and to shorten the transition."[121]

The passions motivating primitive accumulation are not linked with capitalist relations of production proper, but rather with two distinct, antediluvian forms of capital which mature in various socioeconomic formations and are handed down by the Middle Ages: usurer's capital and merchant's capital.[122] Where the other prerequisites of capitalism are present, usury is a powerful lever in introducing it, since money-lending ruins both the feudal lord and the small-scale producer and also centralizes the conditions of labor—that is, builds up independent monetary wealth. Similarly, merchantry centralizes potential industrial capital. Its existence and development are historical premises of capitalist production for this reason; in addition and more importantly, merchantry furthers production for trade and selling on a large scale—it promotes the commodity relations which are indispensible for capitalism. However, its development "is incapable by itself of promoting and explaining the transition from one mode of production to another."[123] That imperative is rooted in the productive forces.

Although capitalist relations of production do not exist in their historically proper (industrial) form, capitalist passions—the worship of private property and the pursuit of profit—are already present in usury and merchantry, and their expansion is capable of sponsoring the tasks of accumulation which *Capital* sets forth. The backdrop to this is the rise of money and exchange as feudalism declines. "Wherever personal relations were superseded by money relations, wherever natural duties gave way to money payments, there bourgeois relations took the place of feudal relations."[124] Bourgeois relations presuppose money relations, along with widespread exchange, universal commodity production, and the stripping of any non-utilitarian dressing from men's production relations. Money relations need not be capitalist relations, but they both invite and are stimulated by the early forms of capital. Here, then, it is necessary to turn to the germination of industrial capital, which is to prosper and spread on this fertile soil.

Although there is an important qualitative difference between commercial and industrial capital, the merchant frequently bridged the two; thus, the *Grundrisse* refers to the "quite simple and obvious ways" in which the merchant's money was often converted into industrial capital.[125] When the merchant either purchases labor-power to produce the commodities which he intends to sell or turns small masters into his middlemen, he ceases to be what he is throughout the Middle Ages, simply a dealer in other people's commodities.[126] This typical transformation of the merchant into an industrial capitalist is matched by another: the evolution, into a merchant and capitalist, of that producer who both purchases his raw materials himself (instead of relying on a merchant to furnish them) and produces not for particular customers but for the world market. Marx calls this "the really revolutionizing path" because the mode of material production overthrows commercial hegemony.[127] Production still needs commerce, of course, but takes it for granted instead of dwelling in subordination to it.

The actual transition, as envisioned by Marx, from feudal production to capitalist production involves this mixing of producers and merchants as well as the occasional appearance of the intermediary "small master"—half-laborer, half-capitalist. The key to capitalist production is the exploitation of wage labor, but a certain minimum amount of capital is needed to ensure that the capitalist producer can hire sufficient workers to liberate himself from manual labor.[128] The first difference from guild production is simply the greater number of workers employed. With the ability of capital to hire any kind of labor and with the extension of business and the accompanying demand of the merchant for more commodities, writes Marx, guild work is driven over its limits and changes formally into capitalist production.[129] Although many artisans or even wage laborers were able to transform themselves through their own industry into small capitalists, the primitive accumulation of potential capital and the creation of a "free" work force greatly accelerated what would otherwise have been the "snail's pace" of capitalism's commencement.[130]

Capitalism eventually succeeds in rooting out guild production, but the guilds themselves are not transmogrified into capitalist bodies. In fact, the earliest manufactures were often obliged to begin production away from the guild towns, with their restrictions on employment and investment. Eventually, the guilds cave in under external capitalist pressure, but only after capitalism's manufactures have harnessed the productive forces which the guilds themselves fetter. This is also a reason why the release of the agricultural population is so important in Marx's story.

If the manner of this transition is not hard to conceive, what exactly precipitates it? The prerequisites are obvious by now: developed commerce and production of commodities, accumulations of money wealth (potential means of production and subsistence), and increasing throngs of laborers divested of the means of production. In addition, there is a development of the productive forces sufficient to support capitalism—a factor absent from ancient Rome. "The general presence of wage labor presupposes a higher development of the productive forces than in the stages preceding wage labor, who denies this?"[131] Indeed, it is doubtful that free labor before the Middle Ages would have been disciplined or skilled enough to support a capitalist class. Furthermore, these productive forces are begging for work relations which can appropriately manage them. Capitalism furnishes these (although it does not immediately tamper with the handicraft basis of production) by organizing manufacture more cooperatively and efficiently, by bringing larger numbers of laborers together, and by elaborating the division of labor within the workshop. Capitalist production seems to sprout prolifically simply because it was inevitable that someone would start making money by hiring labor-power, given the climate of profit consciousness and the ripeness of the productive forces and other material preconditions. Since this allows the entrepreneur to manufacture more efficaciously and more profitably, others are bound to follow. While capitalism does not conquer the economic realm overnight, Marx maintains that commodity production necessarily drives toward capitalist production as soon as the laborer ceases to be part of the conditions of production or of a natural community: capitalist production annuls and lifts up (hebt auf) the individual, independent basis of commodity production to a higher level.[132]

CHAPTER FIVE

Conclusion

THE PURPOSE of this essay has been to explore, thoroughly and carefully, a central but neglected theme of historical materialism: the character and connection of the productive forces and relations of production. The dialectic of their interplay and advance constitutes for Marx the infrastructure of historical evolution; this dynamic provides history with its material unity and pushes it forward. A vista has now been reached from which it should be possible to review the progress of the discussion heretofore, to draw together some of the threads loosed in this investigation, and to reweave these back into the larger context of Marx's thought, thus making more explicit the conclusions and consequences of the present study for the understanding and evaluation of Marx's theory of history.

The Productive-Force Dynamic: A Review

My prime concern has been to present an accurate account of Marx's understanding of the mechanics of historical evolution, both his charting of its concrete course and his abstract, theoretical view of it. Although Marx's complexity and occasional inconsistency bar me from claiming to have proved my interpretation of historical materialism, I do affirm that it most satisfactorily accommodates Marx's general pronouncements and his specific verbal usage, as well as his apparent intentions in both.

Superficial examination shows that the concepts "productive forces" and "relations of production" are crucial to Marx's theory of historical materialism, so it is surprising that their character and interconnection are not widely understood. His theory of historical change and development cannot be fully or satisfactorily expounded until they are explicated. Although Marx never expressly defined these concepts, textual examination reveals how Marx comprehended and employed them. Compared to their more technical brothers in Marx's economic vocabulary, the meaning of these terms is rather loose and flexible, and Marx hardly bound himself to a totally consistent and precise usage. Nonetheless, the concepts are fairly stable and may be plotted with a reasonable degree of accuracy. Such variations as do occur are, generally speaking, intelligible within their context; they do not require that the project of elucidating Marx's words (and his theory) be abandoned or that Marx be credited with either a unique conception of language or a special metaphysic. Incomplete and misleading definitions of these concepts were rejected earlier, and it was argued that Marx's idiom is at least logically unexceptionable. His theoretical ship may not ultimately remain afloat, but its parts fit together and no conceptual ineptness prevents the launching.

The productive forces, it was said, include human labor-power and the means of production. The instruments and objects of labor comprise the means of production; they are the powers which society has at its command in its continuous struggle with nature, in its ongoing material production. Both mental and material, subjective and objective, living and objectified, these productive forces are, for Marx, thoroughly human. They provide the index of man's economic evolution and the material link with both the natural order and the previous history of production. Although Marx does hold, in the sense which has been explicated, a technological-determinist thesis about human history, he would be surprised at what a bugbear this has become—even among his latter-day disciples, many of whom are anxious to exorcise the spectre of machines lording it over human society, which is conjured up in their minds by "technological determinism." Ironically, Marx's interpreters take the alienation of man's productive forces under capitalism and their domination over the direct producers during that epoch as the model of productive-force determinism. As a result, his supporters shy away from the theory while a sturdy group of critics pronounces it untenable. These misinterpretations need not be reviewed again. Notwithstanding the long history of oppressive class societies and the profound estrangement endured by men under capitalism, for Marx the productive forces are human forces, by and large man's creations, employed in his material reproduction of society. Furthermore, only the productive forces, the product of man's most fundamental and distinctively human activity, bear the seeds of true human freedom.

Relations of production link the productive forces with human agents in the process of material production. These production relations were seen to be of different orders, essentially divisible into two genres: work and ownership. They are the relations within which production is carried on: both the actual technical relations which are materially necessary for production to proceed, and the relations which govern the control of the productive forces and the products of production, without which social production could not occur. The social relations of production shape society generally. The postulated explanatory hegemony of these relations, one aspect of man's social existence, over the other spheres of social life, however, does not imply that man's humanity or freedom has been reduced.

When Marx's concepts are unpacked, the conceptual elegance of his theory is evident: as the productive forces develop, the relations of production must change if these forces—both the ones presently employed and those potentially serviceable but unused (as well as materially possible but not yet existent forces)—are to be harnessed adequately in production. Depending on the historical situation under examination, the productive forces will stand in greater or lesser accord with their given work and ownership relations, and the nature and necessity of their compatibility or conflict with those relations will vary. That Marx envisioned a determination of the relations of production by the productive forces was insisted upon in Chapter Two. This determination constitutes a recurrent theme in his writings; indeed, it lies at the heart of his conception of history. There is no warrant to mitigate Marx's belief in this basic paramountcy of the productive forces. Although the march of the productive forces may be propelled to a greater or lesser extent by the particular social frame in which they move, their historical expansion is characterized by a tendency toward development regardless of their social form.* With this advance, the production relations, both ownership and work, change and develop. The productive forces both motivate and provide the foundation for the introduction of new relations.

The development of the productive forces through history tells the story of man's evolving dialectical intercourse with nature. This development, the primacy of which seems for Marx to reside in the basic character of production itself, necessitates adjustments in men's relations to each other and to the productive forces. With these changes in the social relations of production, the rest of the social world alters. Marx is not concerned with particular, individual relations adjusting, but with the pressure exerted by the general character and level of the productive forces on an entire mode of production. Thus, as has been seen, Marx analyzes the logic of a system of production as it reacts to the maturation of man's productive capacities.

As the productive forces improve, alterations in men's work relations are frequently required if the productive possibilities offered by those forces are to be actualized. Other things being equal, the character of the ownership relations of production, of the given mode of production at a certain point in its evolution, will decide whether or not these potential work relations will be effected quickly, slowly, or at all. Often, the required changes

---

*In the Asiatic mode of production, this tendency is largely thwarted; see Chapter Four, pp. 124–29.

are insignificant and can easily be implemented within the framework of the prevailing ownership relations; however, in Marx's view, there occurs a time in a mode of production's phylogeny when such changes can no longer be accommodated or can no longer be accommodated smoothly. The ownership relations of production will then stand in the path of the realization of society's full productive possibilities. This may happen in at least two fashions. First, the ownership relations may prohibit the given work relations from occurring. Thus, for example, guild production was incompatible with the work relations of large-scale manufacture, although the productive forces necessary for the latter were at hand. In such a case, it seems, the type of ownership relations in question may be overthrown or, alternatively, competing ownership relations may spring up, relations which adequately yoke the productive forces.

Second, the new work relations may be established within the old mode of production, but with the result that production is unable to proceed stably within them. The main example of this, of course, is capitalism: it provides the productive forces and the work relations which are suited on the whole to those forces— namely, by organizing large-scale modern industry. These are the work relations which, shorn of their capitalist integument, will provide the productive basis of a socialist society; capitalism, conversely, is unable to manage the productive forces which it has summoned into being. An analogous historical process occurs with the disintegration of primitive communism when private work relations—farm plots worked by individual families—emerge within the shell of communal ownership. This contradictory state of affairs—private work relations, community ownership—may remain for a long time, as Marx noted with regard to the Russian mir.[1] But it is unstable and leads, as in ancient Greece and Rome, to the private ownership of the land, of the means of production, and of the product already worked or produced by the individual.

In other historical periods, the exact location of the conflict between productive forces and relations of production is not clearly designated by Marx. In the emergence of the classical slave mode and then in the development of feudal relations of production, changes in work and ownership relations are intertwined more intimately than in the above examples. While it may not be fruitful to distinguish too rigidly between different configurations of interplay between ownership and work relations, the difficulty in the cases just mentioned, of course, is the absence of a clear discussion by Marx of the nature and developmental inclination of the modes of production in question. It is precisely in terms of such an analysis that the specific productive-force dynamic must be unraveled.

Similarly, the interaction of class struggle with the developmental momentum of each mode of production must be brought out through careful study of each mode. The patterns of class struggle, and of its connection with the interplay between productive forces and relations of production, vary greatly. During the decline of feudalism, a capitalist class emerges and matures through several stages as the type of production with which it is linked evolves, spreads, and changes its position vis à vis the older feudal structure. The bourgeoisie attains a fairly conscious comprehension of itself as the bearer of progress and individual liberty, hostile to the older order; it smites its feudal opponents in order to consolidate and further the capitalist economic relations that have already grown within feudalism and the period of its aftermath.

While feudalism permits the germ of capitalist to flourish within it, the bourgeoisie creates in a much sharper, dialectical fashion its antagonist and eventual destroyer, the proletariat. The working class is the other half of capitalist society, private property's negative side, "its restlessness within its very self."[2] The proletariat strengthens and grows with capital's expansion. Always in resistance, in various ways, to the class which exploits and oppresses it, the proletariat, in contest with the bourgeoisie, steels itself and gains consciousness of its historical position. Eventually the working class must wrestle with the bourgeoisie because it cannot realize the socioeconomic realm, the forging of which is its historic role, until the reign of capital is broken.

Elsewhere, progress is not tightly hitched to the wagon of any one class. During the decline of the slave mode and the emergence of feudalism, no class or classes directly facilitate the transition. Indeed, the Roman class struggle ruins all the contending parties, and the ascendancy of seignorial relations may largely represent the accommodation of older ruling elements to a new productive-force situation—the progress afforded by this new order taking centuries to manifest. Finally, within the era of primitive communism, while the particular type of community depends on the nature of the available productive forces, this is not the fruit of class struggle at all.

Class conflict need not always play midwife to a socio-historical transformation—any more than it is the sine qua non of every alteration of the relations of production. On the other hand, the causes of revolution do not entirely coincide with a discrepancy between the productive forces and their relations. Class relations, and thus antagonism and struggle between classes, are a function of society's relations of production, and the normally latent conflict of classes may well materialize in open battle as a result of specific, local issues. Of course, social boulversement is more likely in a period of opposition between the productive forces and the relations of production. Such an economic contradiction encourages class struggle simply because it poses problems for the smooth and continued functioning of the initial relations.

Since classes are divided by their material interests, during a conflict between the productive forces and their relations they may align themselves on opposing sides of the effort to realize the relations of production appropriate to man's productive possibilities. Where a class triumphs, its success rests on its ability either to sustain the production relations appropriate to the productive forces or to resolve a discrepancy between the two. In real history, as Marx surely acknowledged, class analysis is quite a complicated business, with diverse groups and varying interests to be considered. Despite the complexities of these alignments and the contingent results of any particular class contest, it is the productive forces which set, in the long run, the limit to what can be attained and which determine the relative strength of the bellicose parties. Whether or not class struggle is necessary to acquire a new economic order—just as whether or not any given social upheaval will result in a new mode of production—depends upon the particular, historically specific nexus between the forces and the relations of production.

Persistent Difficulties

The basic historical materialist theme which has been my concern has now been reviewed, but the discussion in previous chapters—and in particular the reconstruction of Marx's reflections on pre-capitalism—have uncovered certain peculiarities in this dynamic of productive forces and relations of production which need to be examined. The first of these is that the early socio-historical transformations described by Marx lack the impetus and the dialectical character of the momentum leading from capitalism to socialism. Only capitalism prompts the development of the forces of production as a direct consequence of its relations of production—so only this social formation finds itself in the uncomfortable position of fettering what it is simultaneously stimulating. Indeed, the conflict of capitalism with its productive forces would seem to have a distinctive claim to the rubric "contradiction."

Marx, of course, does stress the similarity of the conflict of productive forces with their relations of production in all these different modes of production. In addition to the "Preface," consider this passage from the *Grundrisse*:

Beyond a certain point, the development of the productive forces becomes a barrier for capital; hence, the capital relation [becomes] a barrier for the development of the productive forces of labor. When it has reached this point, capital, i.e., wage labor, enters into *the same relation*

towards the development of social wealth and of the forces of production as the guild system, serfdom, slavery, and is necessarily stripped off
as a fetter.[3]

While this emphasizes that pre-capitalist modes of production
come to fetter the productive forces they command, it does not
commit Marx to the view that pre-capitalist social forms both
animate *and* shackle them. Indeed, such a claim would be incompatible with the conservatism attributed by Marx to history's
early social formations.[4] This must be borne in mind in interpreting the sentence from the "Preface" in which Marx refers to
the relations of production turning from forms of development
of the productive forces into their fetters. "Entwicklungsformen
der Produktivkräfte" here could be taken to mean either "forms
which develop the productive forces," or "forms in which the
productive forces develop." The first meaning, which is obviously stronger, reflects the contradictory dynamic between productive forces and relations of production which powers the
transformation from capitalism to socialism; but only the second
rendering reconciles the "Preface" to Marx's conception of pre-
capitalist development.

Even if the more reasonable though weaker interpretation is
adopted, the strength of the productive-force impulse under
capitalism toward socialism still appears exceptional. No other
transition so happily accords with the "Preface."[5] While Marx
thought it important to stress the overriding parallels between
the development of these earlier modes and the process which
he examined in *Das Kapital*, one cannot help feeling that in the
"Preface" he was, to some extent, reading back into previous
world history the contradiction which he perceived between the
productive forces and relations of capitalism. Marx himself
weakens this model when he engages in his actual historical
studies of the pre-capitalist era.

A second point regarding Marx's analysis of pre-capitalist
modes of production, which needs to be drawn out here, concerns the conspicuous affinity of the "natural" economies, de-

spite their apparent diversity. While these societal forms differ greatly, by contrast with capitalism their productive capacities are all equally low. It is far from obvious that the systems of production which Marx identifies (slave, Asiatic, feudal) can be accounted for, primarily, by differences between their respective productive forces. While these social types are indeed dissimilar (culturally, politically, and so on), it seems doubtful, first, that the differences in their actual manner of producing (essentially, they all involve tillage of the land by a subaltern class) are significant enough to generate their manifest social contrasts; and second, that even if this were so, their respective productive forces vary enough to explain their divergent modes of production. These and similar difficulties should have been apparent in the review of Marx's historical narratives in Chapter Four, and need not be embroidered here. However, they are empirical issues, not really problems of abstract analysis, and Marx's position could be affirmed by further socio-historical research, and consequent theoretical elaboration, demonstrating the links of dependency from these pre-capitalist societies to their respective modes of production and productive forces.

A problem of a more theoretical nature concerns whether, or in what sense, these modes of production have distinct developmental tendencies. In principle, it seems that no non-market society could have an economic momentum at all comparable in its autonomy and constancy to that of capitalism; that is, it seems that only market societies have economic regularities which recur regardless of the intentions of individuals (this is not to say, regardless of their behavior). Precisely these are what make economic science, and political economy, possible. By contrast, economic events in the natural economies depend very much on inclinations and decisions of individuals (such as whether or not to raise rent) which are not always or even usually a function of previous economic events beyond their control, as is the case in a market situation. Indeed, Marx allows that only in capitalism is the economic realm functionally autonomous, while in earlier societies economic relations are interwoven with relations of personal (noneconomic) domination and subordination. Thus, it seems that the evolutionary necessity (if any) of the pre-capitalist modes of production must be very different from the pure economic logic of capitalism; but what their "political economy" would look like, or in what sense their relations of production do have an internal socioeconomic impulse, Marx never really divulged.

It could, of course, be the case that the evolutionary momentum of these social formations is simply the consequence of progress in the productive-force domain alone. For Marx there had to be some underlying developmental necessity to history or else historiography could never be scientific, but this need not imply that earlier social formations bear a systemic evolutionary logic analogous to capitalism's tendency toward industrial concentration and centralization. Whether or not they are analogous obviously has consequences for the interpretation of Marx's historical schema. On the one hand, if Marx believed that these earlier modes of production were characterized by an internal, developmental socioeconomic dynamic, like that of capitalism, then there is a striking absence of evidence for this in his writings (which are already too speculative with regard to the period of pre-capitalist society). On the other hand, if the only evolutionary impulse is provided by the expansion of the productive forces (and this would be, to some extent, exogenous with respect to the mode of production itself), then the necessity of the specific historical sequence preceding capitalism is weakened. Of course, it could still be a result of productive-force developments, but in that case Marx would not be affirming, for instance, that slavery *always* prefaces feudalism or feudalism *inherently* leads to capitalism. There would not be the internal, dialectical link between these systems that there is between capitalism and socialism.

More likely, perhaps (especially if the Eurocentricity of Marx's historical studies is transcended), is that the different forms of economic organization in the pre-capitalist period intersect and blend in history, instead of marking general economic epochs.[6] The ideal types which Marx postulates may, in fact, provide a useful sociological heuristic.* But they hardly seem to capture the multiplicity of economic forms in mankind's development—as Marx himself seems to acknowledge: "Between the full development of this foundation of industrial society [i.e., the emergence of exchange relations—WHS] and the patriarchal condition, many intermediate stages, endless nuances [occur]."[7] Yet, it is this very diversity which is ignored in the classification of socioeconomic epochs offered by the "Preface." That in itself is tolerable, given the function of organizing concepts, but the vision of these modes of production evolving internally into their successors (as capitalism transmutes into socialism) makes accounting for these "endless nuances" very much more difficult simply because it subordinates the actual productive dialectic of particular societies too much to the supposed developmental pattern of the "Preface" modes.[8] Marx, of course, wishes to interpret empirical history through theoretical spectacles, but if a proper balance is not found between the "real" and its presumed theoretical "ideal," the understanding of historical development can be greatly hindered. The theoretical model, as Marx admits in principle, must be drawn from history —not imposed upon it.

More instructive patterns might well be discerned in human economic development, models which do not break history into segregated social epochs,[9] and Marx himself, while always stressing the variety of forms of human socioeconomic organization, occasionally falls back on the more fundamental, slightly looser contrast between monetary and capitalist economies, on the one hand, and natural economies, comprised by seemingly personal ties, on the other: "Relations of personal dependence . . . are the first social forms. . . . Personal independence founded on *objective* dependence [i.e., capitalism—WHS] is the second great

---

*Lest the pessimistic observations of this and the following section should seem to undermine completely the benefits of adopting Marx's perspective, the reader should consult Ernest Gellner's favorable review of the current state of Soviet anthropology, which bases itself on Marx's "Preface" typology. (Gellner, "The Soviet and the Savage," *Times Literary Supplement*, October 18, 1974.)

form. . . . Free individuality, based on the universal development of individuals and on their subordination to their communal, social productivity as their social wealth, is the third
stage."[10]

Here, as in other places, Marx is concerned to highlight the
prominent features of capitalism against both the common backdrop of its predecessors and the radically different society of
its inferred successor. The very strength of the contrast between
capitalism and the "first social forms" undermines the tenability
of a five-stage model, with each stage the necessary prerequisite
of its sequel. Capitalism marks such a clean break with prior
forms of social production that it is hard to picture it as just
another way-station on the road to socialism.

As the productive forces advance, according to historical materialism, they achieve the relations of production which best
harness them and ensure their continued progress. It might well
be the case, however, that the level of productive development
sets only general limits to the economic forms it brings about,
dividing them simply into the following progressive epochs:
pre-class society, pre-capitalist class society, capitalist society, and
post-class society.[11] Despite its apparent generality, the explanatory power of such a thesis (if true) would be great. Within such
stages, in particular in the era of pre-capitalist class society, qualitative differences between productive forces of a similar level
could be called upon by Marx's theory to explain social variations—for Marx would surely not have abandoned a "materialist" analysis of the "endless nuances" of history.

By contrast, a too-limited categorization of history and a too-
rigid model of its evolutionary pattern (antagonism, overthrow,
stabilization) do render such a project more difficult. This
point has long been urged against "vulgar" Marxists who take
the "Preface" stages as the last word on history, but it must be
acknowledged that such a model has the support of certain of
Marx's pronouncements and that rejection of it (as being too
unsubtle a reading of Marx) is often accompanied by a repudia-
tion of Marx's (logically separable) belief in the primacy of the

productive forces over the relations of production. It bears re-
peating, however, that this model does not necessarily follow
from Marx's more fundamental belief "that as men develop
their productive faculties, that is, as they live, they develop certain relations with one another and that the nature of these relations must necessarily change with the change and growth of the
productive faculties."[12] This thesis hardly entails that history can
be periodized into determinate self-evolving modes of production, still less that these are the ones which Marx suggests. One
might well follow Marx in his productive-force determinism and
nevertheless trace out a different model of pre-capitalist development.

Toward an Evaluation

The present study has been undertaken within the framework
of Marx's thought and has attempted to excavate and elaborate
certain neglected aspects of historical materialism, centering on
the dynamics of historical development and the function of Produktivkräfte and Produktionsverhältnisse within this. Such an
exegetical exercise should serve to clarify one's understanding of
a thinker: to elucidate his dominant problematic, to delineate its
themes, and to bring to light both inconsistencies within, and
further consequences of, his work. Despite its utility, a study of
this type hardly provides an empirical rule against which the
claims of a theorist like Marx must be measured. Textual examination is only the first step in the evaluation of an author who
advances bold empirical propositions about history and society.
In this concluding section, I wish to clarify some of the issues
involved in the project of delivering a judgment on Marx.

Marx and Engels advanced the different themes of historical
materialism largely in opposition to the idealist currents then
prevalent, all of which portrayed historical advance as, in some
fashion or other, the consequence of the development of the
human spirit (or some analogue). Contemporary historians,
while happily abandoning both the narration of kings and bat-
tles and transhistorical speculation for the study of "social condi-

tions," are, nonetheless, inclined to perceive the "idealism-materialism" opposition in historiography as a dead end; why should historical progress be supposed to be a function of either type of "factors"? However, while these alternatives may not be exhaustive, this fails to show that certain seemingly fundamental questions, such as "Why is there progress in history?" and "In what does it consist?", to which these grander conceptions of history addressed themselves, are unworthy of discussion.

In his answer to such queries, Marx stresses the dominant role of material production in structuring society and argues that the development of mankind can be interpreted as a succession of necessary responses to its expanding productive capacity, which is itself the natural product of man's ontologically and biologically fundamental encounter with nature. The development of man's productive forces provides the unity of history and explains the basic contour of its evolution. Like its idealist rivals, historical materialism organizes the investigation of history by focusing the energy of the researcher in a particular direction, by raising certain questions, and by accepting only certain types of answers. Marx's theory of history and society serves as a heuristic, offering a bold and all-embracing general perspective on man's existence and evolution. I have said that the thesis of productive-force determinism is empirical; but is it not, as many have supposed, simply part of a larger metaphysical view of society, which can be neither proved nor disproved?

Although Marx and Engels intended in *The German Ideology* to overthrow all a priori frameworks and to return to the real, material world of empirical individuals, what they thought they were doing there appears to the contemporary observer to have differed from what they were actually doing. Instead of being able to abandon all preconceptions in history, the two German iconoclasts only tender an alternative world-view, which —despite its attractions—is more speculative and quite a bit less empirical than they imagined. Even so, while the thesis of productive-force determinism appears to presuppose a certain conception of man, labor, and nature (though Marx's specific assumptions are not entirely clear, as shown in Chapter Two), it does make a claim about the way things are, a claim which appears, in principle, to be falsifiable. If it is true that the materialist conception of history involves both empirical and non-empirical aspects, this need not be an unusual or even unsatisfactory state of affairs. Scientific theory is not necessarily rendered untenable because of metaphysical elements; in fact, their presence may be not only unavoidable but scientifically helpful.[13] What is important are the empirical claims and models offered by the theory, what it reveals about the world, the predictions it fosters, and the scientific progress it encourages.* To say this is hardly to demean science or to open the floodgates of irrationalism.

In fact, Marxism is frequently incriminated, in accord with the above, for lacking any real predictive or explanatory power, for being compatible with any future state of affairs. Usually, this criticism is leveled against Marxist political theory, which indeed seems explanatorily lame. Whether this charge can be more accurately lodged against scholarly Marxist work in history or economics, for example, than against the social sciences in general is debatable, but the issue here is whether the thesis of productive-force determinism itself satisfies this fundamentally scientific criterion of empirical falsifiability.

The main difficulty in testing this hypothesis lies in the fact that any explanation or prediction of a particular historical transformation for Marx is accomplished in terms of a theory of the relevant modes of production. The thesis of productive-

*Unfortunately, this stirs up a hornets' nest of philosophical issues. Let me say, briefly, that I do not intend, by claiming that there are non-empirical elements within the corpus of scientific knowledge (either as residues of metaphysical thought or as part of its necessary conceptual apparatus), to imply that science cannot be demarcated from non-science, metaphysics, ideology, and so on. Rather, the suggestion is that the function and consequences of a theory may be more important than the evaluation of the logical status of its component parts (as, say, verifiable or not) in determining its scientific character. Unlike some contemporary Marxists, I do not think the scientific status of Marxism (if indeed it were scientific) is something which could be demonstrated or guaranteed in a purely formal fashion. They also forget that the scientific character of a theory does not entail its truth.

force determinism, while it may serve as a heuristic, does not generate a theory of a given society's economic relations. Of course, Marx would not have envisioned that the formulation of an accurate theory could occur without a commitment to the predominant role of the productive forces in the determination of society's economic relations, but I am simply pointing out that the accuracy of Marx's account of any particular historical transition depends upon more than the single premise of productive-force determinism. For example, Marx's prediction of socialism does not rest solely on the determining role of the productive forces, but also on a thesis about capitalism's projected ability to manage their advance. The failure of socialism to occur in the advanced capitalist nations may only show that Marx underestimated the ability of capitalism to accommodate the development of the productive forces, and not that the productive forces are not determining of their mode of production. Demonstration of the incorrectness of one of Marx's historical narratives or predictions is not sufficient to snap, by virtue of modus tollens, the "guiding thread" of productive-force determinism.

In addition, the testability of the thesis is diminished by the elastic time interval which Marx allows for the adjustment of the relations of production to the advance of the productive forces, by the antagonistic character he attributes to progress in general, and by the fact that any real social formation may only imperfectly embody a given mode of production. Marx did wish to provide material explanations for these theoretically permitted discrepancies and delays in the determination of a mode of production by the development of man's productive capacity, but this does not force the theory into a position in which it can be neatly falsified. Although Marx has been impeached for this, it shall be clear below why such an elaboration of a scientific theory is not, ipso facto, in bad faith.

To rebut Marx's thesis of the determining role of the productive forces one would have to tender a more viable theory of a particular historical transition, one which showed that the development of the productive forces was not responsible for a change in the mode of production. Of course, one need not accept the remainder of Marx's perspective in order to refute his technological determinism, but one is required to offer a more intelligent explanation of the general developments which fall under Marx's scrutiny (for example, the rise of capitalism).

This might seem like an unreasonable requirement. After all, one might ask, why should it not suffice to show that Marx is wrong without being obliged to offer a competing theory? Indeed, a Popperian would request that Marx himself stipulate the conditions which would show his theory to be false, without waiting for it to be supplanted by a superior one. This is given added weight by the sentiment that the very project of formulating such a general theory of history is ill-conceived.

It is true that the twentieth century has been infertile ground for historical theories of the kind which Marx offers. The timidity of historians in venturing from their specializations to offer more catholic reflection on the course and nature of historical development does not, however, show that such queries cannot be braved. Both historians and ordinary men constantly seek and are satisfied with explanations in history. If one does not forbid such question as "Why did the Roman empire decline?" or "Why did feudalism arise in Europe?"—and there seems to be no reason to do this—then why should one rule out larger questions, like "Why do social formations in general rise and fall?" Now, it may be either that Marx designated the wrong constellation of factors as explanatorily primary, or that large-scale historical changes are so complex that it would be absurd to single out any one set of elements as dominant; thus Marx's theory would not succeed in offering a viably empirical, general view of history. However, this is a matter for research to determine; it has yet to be shown either that the broad issue of why society progresses should be abandoned or that Marx's answer is wrong.

The above does not yet suffice to show that one should cling to the best answers one may have until a better theory is produced. After all, Popper requires scientists to specify which possible states of the world would falsify their theories, to engage in crucial experiments, and to reject their hypotheses when they fail empirical test. Recently, however, it has been persuasively argued that this is neither the way science has operated in the past nor the best way for it to proceed in the future.[14] Scientists, it is suggested, do not abandon their theories when faced with (possible) counterexamples and anomalies; indeed, all theories are born with these, and often it is only with time and the success of the theory in other fields that these can be solved (if at all). This tenacity is to be applauded. Ad hoc defenses and the refusal to recognize alleged counter-instances as decisive refutations of the theory allow the theory (or more technically, in Lakatos's language, the "hard core" of the research program) to retain its momentum, to grow, and to offer new insights. Attention focuses on the positive and progressive results of the research program, not on its theoretical inconsistencies and anomalies. Further: "There is no falsification before the emergence of a better theory."[15] The question becomes one of whether or not the research program is capable of generating novel theories, predicting fresh facts, and stimulating new research—that is, whether the program is progressive or degenerating.

With regard to the theory of historical materialism and the thesis of productive-force determinism, this has important consequences. It intimates why it is not sufficient merely to outline defects in Marx's account of historical development. An alternative conception, showing that the productive forces are not or cannot be determining, must be worked out. Although there are clear difficulties in Marx's theory of history, some of which are discussed in the last section, and much of his specific historical narrative has been surpassed by a hundred years of additional research, there is no real rival theory of history. The comparative backwardness of the social and historical sciences thus leads to a paradox. Although Marx's theory could hardly be said to meet even Lakatos's relaxed requirements for qualifying as a progressive and energetic research program, one is in the predicament of being stuck with this apparently deteriorating paradigm, owing to the absence of a theoretical replacement.

If only for this reason, Marx's theory of history, of the determining role of the development of man's productive capacity, cannot be simply dismissed—not without the presentation of a more suitable account or a demonstration of the infeasibility of the type of project Marx is undertaking (one which establishes the limits of his program). The paradox above could hardly compel the researcher to adopt Marx's perspective, but it does argue that those who do cannot be slighted for so doing.

It is entirely possible, of course, that Marx's deterministic theorem might be found to hold only within certain limits or for specific periods. Many of the putative laws of social science, even those which are most highly respected, suffer from clear counter-instances—that is, from exceptions for which the laws themselves do not account. Similarly, Marx's theory may be a useful generalization, even if not universally applicable. Its demonstrated deficiencies, then, would spur the study of its limiting conditions and this, hopefully, would produce either a rigorously stated law of restricted scope (replacing a vague generalization with exceptions) or an alternative theory into which Marx's genuine insights could be incorporated.[16]

Such a limitation of the applicability of historical materialism would undermine the unifying, technological vision Marx offers of history. This might well be a loss, but no one can advocate accepting a false perspective merely for its aesthetic and comforting qualities. On the other hand, if Marx's theory of history were to gain support from historical research, if progress were made in its theoretical elaboration, if fertile research were stimulated, then the unifying vision of Marxism might be an additional virtue. If all theories are allowed to compete, then it is to their results that one must attend. I have argued that Marx's theory of history, despite its problems, offers a plausible vehicle for social and historical research. Marxian theorists may not be in chains, but they still have a world to win.

Notes

Notes

Complete authors' names, titles, and publication data are given in the Bibliography, pp. 191–97. Abbreviations used in these notes are:

AS	Morgan, *Ancient Society*
Cap.	Marx, *Capital*
Dietz	Marx, *Grundrisse der Kritik der Politischen Ökonomie* (published by Dietz Verlag)
EN	Marx, *The Ethnological Notebooks*
Grundrisse	Marx, *Grundrisse* (Penguin ed., in English)
PCEF	Marx, *Pre-Capitalist Economic Formations*
"Resultate"	Marx, "Resultate des Unmittelbaren Produktions-prozesses"
SW	Marx and Engels, *Selected Works*
TSV	Marx, *Theories of Surplus Value*

Introduction

1. I shall use "Marx's theory of history," "historical materialism," and "the materialist conception of history" as synonyms. I treat them as blanket terms for a welter of claims and hypotheses in Marx's work, and by saying "theory of history" I do not of course mean to imply that Marx's materialist conception constitutes a rigorously formulated body of propositions, comparable to the formalized theories of natural science. Also, in this study I do not attempt to mold the different aspects of historical materialism into such a systematic theory, nor do I try to segregate it formally from other aspects of Marx's thought (such as dialectical materialism). I leave the boundaries between Marx's conception of history and his other ideas at an intuitive level.

2. The term "fundamentalist" is from Bertell Ollman (who derives it from John Plamenatz). See his *Alienation*, pp. 6–8. The above polemic is

delivered, in part, against commentators like Ollman. The reader is invited to furnish other examples.

Chapter One

1. *Werke,* 13: 639–40 (*Critique*, p. 215, translation modified). Here, as throughout this essay, the emphasis is that of the quoted author unless stated otherwise. In all works quoted, British spellings have been changed to American.

2. Ollman, p. 41.

3. *Cap.* 2: 33.

4. *Cap.* 2: 83; see *Cap.* 3: 41. "Means of production" and "labor-power" are, respectively, the objective and subjective factors of production. *Cap.* 1: 184, 209.

5. *PCEF*, p. 67 (Dietz, p. 375).

6. The Moore-Aveling translation of *Cap.* 1 and the Moscow translations of *Cap.* 2 and 3 render Arbeitsgegenstände as "objects of labor" as well as "subjects of labor." Although both expressions refer to the things labored on, I find the first phrase less ambiguous and have tried to be consistent in using it.

7. *Cap.* 2: 164 (*Werke* 24: 162); translation modified in accord with note 6. *Cap.* 3: 41 (*Werke* 25: 51).

8. *Cap.* 1: 179–80; on land as an instrument of labor, see *Poverty*, p. 164 (also quoted at *TSV* 2: 158–59); *SW* 3: 15; *PCEF*, pp. 81, 67, 69 (Dietz, pp. 384, 375, 376). The soil in the virgin state in which it supplies man with necessaries ready to hand, however, is said by Marx to be "the universal subject [Gegenstand] of human labor" (*Cap.* 1: 178).

9. *Cap.* 2: 165 (*Werke* 24: 163).

10. *Cap.* 2: 144 (*Werke* 24: 143).

11. "Resultate," p. 30 (ms. p. 465). This is an important (but neglected) partial draft of *Capital*.

12. *Cap.* 1: 203; see *Grundrisse*, pp. 298–300. This distinction is reflected in the one between fixed capital and circulating capital. *Cap.* 2: 164–65. Elsewhere, however, Marx obscures this point; see *Grundrisse* (reference is to Penguin edition unless indicated otherwise), pp. 680–81 (Dietz, p. 572).

13. *Cap.* 2, p. 162 (*Werke* 24: 160). At *TSV* 1: 412, Marx claims that in transportation "a material change is effected in the object of labor—a *spatial* change, a change of place." Elsewhere, transportation is reasoned to be a realm of material production because it is an integral part of the total production of a material thing. *Cap.* 2: 153 (*Werke* 24: 151); *Grundrisse*, pp. 533–34.

14. *Werke* 23: 193; see *Grundrisse*, p. 691.

15. *Grundrisse*, p. 521n. This is the opinion of the translator, but one doubts whether Marx was consistent in this usage. He was not later; see *Werke* 23: 630 (*Cap.* 1: 603).

16. *Cap.* 1: 181; see *TSV* 1: 135–36. Notice the difficulty which Marx

has in remaining true to his own terminology: "Raw material may either form the principal substance of a product, or it may enter into its formation only as an accessory. An accessory may be consumed by the instruments of production . . . or it may be *mixed with the raw material*." *Cap.* 1: 181 (*Werke* 23: 196, my emphasis). The hint is that "true" raw materials are principal substances (p. 181, n. 3), and Marx frequently (although perhaps only inadvertently) contrasts raw materials and auxiliaries. *Cap.* 1: 209, 213; *Cap.* 2: 162; Marx to Engels, August 2, 1862.

17. *Cap.* 1: 181; also, *Cap.* 2: 162.

18. *Cap.* 2: 162–63 (*Werke* 24: 160).

19. *Cap.* 1: 182; see *Grundrisse*, pp. 716–17n.

20. *Grundrisse*, p. 706 (Dietz, p. 594); see *TSV* 3: 266–67.

21. *PCEF*, p. 105 (Dietz, p. 402); see *Grundrisse*, p. 223 (Dietz, p. 135).

22. *TSV* 1: 70 (*Werke* 26.1: 41).

23. Karl Korsch, *Karl Marx*, p. 200. Unfortunately this is not an uncommon error; for another example, see Geoffrey Pilling, "The Law of Value in Ricardo and Marx," p. 291.

24. *Poverty*, p. 174 (*Misère de la Philosophie*, p. 250).

25. *SW* 1: 42–43; but see *Grundrisse*, p. 543 (Dietz, p. 442).

26. *Cap.* 1: 167 (*Werke* 23: 181).

27. *Cap.* 1: 202 (*Werke* 23: 217); see also p. 215n (229n).

28. *Cap.* 1: 178 (*Werke* 23: 193); see *Grundrisse*, p. 300 (Dietz, p. 208). At *Grundrisse*, p. 274 (Dietz, p. 185), Marx appears to designate labor activity as a Produktivkraft, but it will become clear below why it is labor-power—not simply labor—which for Marx is part of the productive forces.

29. For example, *Werke* 24: 42.

30. *Cap.* 1: 339 (*Werke* 23: 359).

31. *SW* 1: 38.

32. *Cap.* 1: 574 (*Werke* 23: 599); see *TSV* 3: 266–67, 294–95.

33. See Marx to Annenkov, December 28, 1846, at *SW* 1: 518.

34. See *Cap.* 1: 621; *Werke* 6: 540; *Poverty*, p. 221 ("On the Question of Free Trade"): the worker's "existence has no other value than that of a simple productive force, and the capitalist treats him accordingly."

35. *Cap.* 3: 259.

36. "Resultate," p. 60 (ms. p. 469e); *TSV* 3: 362. For a contrary assessment, see John McMurtry, "Making Sense of Economic Determinism," p. 251, n. 17.

37. *Grundrisse*, p. 675 (Dietz, p. 567). Marx distinguishes "productive consumption" from "individual consumption," but a capitalist who required his workers to eat while laboring would break down the contrast to some extent; see *Cap.* 1: 572–73.

38. *Cap.* 1: 382 (*Werke* 23: 402–3); see *SW* 1: 93.

39. *Cap.* 1: 361 (*Werke* 23: 383); also *TSV* 2: 234.

40. *SW* 1: 75.

41. *Cap.* 1: 487–88 (*Werke* 23: 511–12).

42. *SW* 3: 19. The *Grundrisse* likewise foresees under communism "the total, universal development of the productive forces of the individual" (p. 515; Dietz, p. 415).

43. M. M. Bober, *Karl Marx's Interpretation of History*, p. 21. Similarly, Karl Federn finds this a problem in *The Materialist Conception of History*, pp. 7–12, as does John Plamenatz, *Man and Society*, Vol. 2, pp. 290–93.

44. *Grundrisse*, p. 540 (Dietz, p. 439).

45. *Cap.* 3: 104 (*Werke* 25: 114); Marx distinguishes there between "universal labor" and "cooperative labor."

46. *TSV* 1: 392; see p. 353.

47. *Cap.* 1: 361 (*Werke* 23: 382); see *Grundrisse*, p. 693. Marx writes at *TSV* 3: 443: "Capitalist production leads to a separation of *science from labor* and at the same time to the use of science in material production."

48. *Cap.* 1: 331–32; *Cap.* 3: 383–84; *TSV* 3: 496; also see Engels' "On Authority" in *SW* 2.

49. *Cap.* 2: 359–60 (*Werke* 24: 356); see *Cap.* 3: 745; *TSV* 3: 182 (*Werke* 26.3: 182). *The Holy Family*, p. 72, credits Proudhon with being the first to draw attention to the gratuitous appropriation of the collective power of labor by capital.

50. *Cap.* 1: 333, 606–7. Marx says that there is a kind of fetishism, similar to that which attaches to money, in the fact that the productive forces of social labor appear as the productive forces of capital. *TSV* 1: 389 (*Werke* 26.1: 365); see *SW* 1: 74. This appearance has an objective basis in that under capitalism "the social spirit of labor obtains an objective existence separate from the individual workers." *Grundrisse*, p. 529n (Dietz, p. 428n).

51. "Resultate," pp. 128–30 (ms. p. 481).

52. The formulation of this distinction between the process of cooperation (an organization of production) and the principle of cooperation (a piece of technical knowledge which is resident in someone's labor-power) was suggested to me by G. A. Cohen. The former is a relation of production; the latter is part of the productive forces.

53. *Cap.* 2: 144 (*Werke* 24: 143); see *Grundrisse*, p. 770 (Dietz, p. 656); *Cap.* 1: 623 (*Werke* 23: 652); *SW* 2: 74. See also *Cap.* 1: 386 (*Werke* 23: 407), which both Gordon Leff and Karl Korsch use to identify the organization of labor as a productive force. Leff, pp. 142–43; Korsch, pp. 198–99.

54. *Cap.* 3: 247 (*Werke* 25: 257).

55. This was drawn to my attention by G. A. Cohen. See Mill at *Cap.* 1: 599 (*Werke* 23: 626).

56. See especially Etienne Balibar's "The Basic Concepts of Historical Materialism," in Louis Althusser and Etienne Balibar, *Reading Capital*, for an explication of this position. Its best defense is in Mahov and Frish, eds., *Society and Economic Relations*.

57. Mahov and Frish argue for (1) and (2). Balibar defends (2) and is implicitly committed to (3) by his and Althusser's denial of the primacy

of the productive forces in Marx. Ben Brewster asserts (3) in his "Introduction to Lukács on Bukharin." Brewster claims authority for his position in Georg Lukács, but I find this uncertain; see Lukács's 1925 review of Bukharin's *Historical Materialism* (reprinted by Brewster; also in Lukács's *Political Writings, 1919–20*).

58. See Mahov and Frish, esp. pp. 28–31.

59. *Grundrisse*, pp. 715, 747, 703 (Dietz, pp. 603, 633, 591); on "already produced productive forces," see *TSV* 2: 538; *SW* 1: 149; *Cap.* 3: 247.

60. *Poverty*, p. 133; also, *SW* 1: 64.

61. *Poverty*, p. 78, and pp. 99–100 (*Misère*, p. 140).

62. *TSV* 1: 389–90 (*Werke* 26.1: 365–66).

63. *TSV* 1: 391 (*Werke* 26.1: 366).

64. Leff, p. 144.

65. *Ibid.*, p. 142.

66. *SW* 1: 159.

67. G. A. Cohen, "On Some Criticisms of Historical Materialism," p. 126.

68. See the "Preface" to *The Critique*; *Poverty*, p. 110; *Cap.* 3: 818 (*Werke* 25: 826–27); *SW* 1: 160; cf. *TSV* 1: 285.

69. Plamenatz, *Man and Society*, Vol. 2, pp. 279–80.

70. *SW* 1: 111.

71. *Cap.* 2: 37 (*Werke* 24: 42); cf. *TSV* 3: 444 (*Werke* 26.3: 437).

72. *Cap.* 1: 486–87 (*Werke* 23: 510–11); see also "Resultate," p. 120.

73. "Resultate," p. 118 (ms. p. 477).

74. *Poverty*, p. 133.

75. *Cap.* 3: 830 (*Werke* 25: 838).

76. See Althusser and Balibar, p. 201.

77. *Cap.* 1: 298 (*Werke* 23: 315), emphasis added; this usage is repeated several times there and on p. 322 (341). See also *Grundrisse*, pp. 585–86 (Dietz, p. 480), *TSV* 3: 383, and the references in Michael Evans, p. 181, n. 98.

78. *Cap.* 3: 263 (*Werke* 25: 273), emphasis added.

79. *Cap.* 1: 35 (emphasis added, and punctuation amended per *Werke* 23: 49). Sometimes, "mode of production" refers to both the social *and* the technical aspects of producing; for example, *Grundrisse*, pp. 97–98 (Dietz, pp. 18–19); *Cap.* 3: 878; *TSV* 3: 491.

80. *PCEF*, pp. 87–88 (Dietz, pp. 389–90).

81. Against this John Arthur would argue that the *social* character of production requires that work relations incorporate at least *two* human agents. This has the unhappy consequence, however, that in a society based on simple commodity production, where each denizen produces independently with his own tools, there would be no work relations at all. See Arthur, pp. 57–60.

82. *Poverty*, p. 133; see *Cap.* 1: 386.

83. Acton, *What Marx Really Said*, pp. 54–55.

84. *Cap.* 1: 382–83 (*Werke* 23: 403). It should be noted that a change

in work relations, as required by the productive forces, can also react back on the labor-power and means of production which they harness. See p. 336 (356) and p. 341 (361).

85. In a symposium with G. A. Cohen, "On Some Criticisms," p. 143 (Acton's emphasis).

86. *Cap.* 1: 196n (*Werke* 25: 210n).

87. *Cap.* 1: 509 (*Werke* 23: 532). While capitalism can manifest itself in the sphere of immaterial production, Marx thought the extent to which it does so was limited and insignificant enough to be ignored safely. *TSV* 1: 410–11. For a discussion of these and related issues, see Ian Gough, "Productive and Unproductive Labour in Marx."

88. Dahrendorf, p. 21.

89. *Cap.* 3: 793 (*Werke* 25: 801). The serf probably did not possess all the means of production with which he worked.

90. Thus, Ernest Mandel is inaccurate when he refers to a "fundamental characteristic of feudalism, namely, *private ownership* of the land by the feudal nobility" (p. 127, note 35). Ernest Untermann, on the other hand, says that the serfs owned the land (p. 139).

91. *On the Paris Commune*, p. 160; see *SW* 1: 306, 276–77, 481–82; *SW* 2: 330; *PCEF*, p. 115 (Dietz, p. 410); *The General Council of the First International 1868–1870. Minutes*, Vol. 3 (July 6, 1869). On their attitude to the peasantry, see Engels' "The Peasant Question in France and Germany" (*SW* 3), and Henry Mayer, esp. pp. 111–12.

92. *Cap.* 3: 676, 797 (*Werke* 25: 688, 805). Similarly, Engels mentions peasants being turned into serfs "first in fact, and then juridically as well." *Peasant War in Germany*, p. 156 (*Werke* 21: 240).

93. *Cap.* 1: 717.

94. *Cap.* 1: 217 (*Werke* 23: 231).

95. *Cap.* 3: 791 (*Werke* 25: 799).

96. *Poverty*, p. 154; see *Revolutions of 1848*, p. 250.

97. *SW* 1: 521 (letter to Annenkov). At *Grundrisse*, p. 88 (Dietz, p. 9) Marx adds that "every form of production creates its own legal relations."

98. See Cohen, "On Some Criticisms," pp. 130–31.

99. *SW* 1: 521, my emphasis.

100. *Cap.* 1: 615n (*Werke* 23: 643n). Y. Varga, the Russian economist, to the contrary, inveighs against the distinction between legal property relations and production relations in the name of dialectics (pp. 338–39).

101. *Werke* 23: 99. (This is a more literal translation than *Cap.* 1: 84.) See also *Werke* 19: 377.

102. *Poverty*, p. 154.

103. *SW* 1: 25, 79–80; *SW* 3: 371, 492–93; *SW* 2: 365; *German Ideology*, pp. 406–7. Cf. Althusser and Balibar, pp. 229–30.

104. *Cap.* 3: 793 (*Werke* 25: 801); see Engels, *The Condition of the Working Class in England*, p. 253.

105. *Cap.* 3: 776 (*Werke* 25: 784); see *Cap.* 2: 32.

106. *PCEF*, p. 92 (Dietz, p. 393).

107. *Cap.* 3: 340 (*Werke* 25: 352). Marx continues: "Slavery on the basis of capitalist production is unjust; likewise fraud in the quality of commodities." See *SW* 2: 365–66 and *SW* 3: 19.

108. *Cap.* 2: 31; *Cap.* 3: 878–79.

109. Marx to J. B. Schweitzer, January 24, 1868 (his emphasis).

110. *Cap.* 1: 574 (*Werke* 23: 599); see *The Holy Family*, p. 69.

111. *Cap.* 1: 77 (*Werke* 23: 91–92); see *Grundrisse*, pp. 163–64 (Dietz, p. 81); *Cap.* 3: 876 (*Werke* 25: 883).

112. *SW* 1: 421.

113. *SW* 1: 47; see *TSV* 1: 285.

114. *Cap.* 1: 301 (translation modified per *Werke* 23: 319); see *Cap.* 1: 653 (*Werke* 23: 683).

115. See *Cap.* 1: 10 (*Werke* 23: 16). Thus, the capitalist, for example, is conceived only as the representative or personification of capital; see, for example, *Cap.* 1: 152 (*Werke* 23: 167); *Grundrisse*, p. 634 (Dietz, p. 528).

116. *Cap.* 1: 298n (315n).

117. *SW* 2: 312–13, 187; Engels, *Anti-Dühring*, pp. 316, 204–5, 207; *SW* 1: 92–93. Greed would seem to be the suppressed premise in Engels' argument if the possibility of class rule is to turn into its actuality; see *SW* 3: 333, and Chapter Four, note 25.

118. *Poverty*, p. 61; *SW* 3: 85, 333; *TSV* 3: 97–98; *The German Ideology*, p. 487. See *Cap.* 3: 819, and *Grundrisse*, pp. 325, 634, on the civilizing mission of capital.

119. See *Cap.* 1: 577–78 (*Werke* 23: 603–4); *TSV* 3: 507–8, 514.

120. *Cap.* 1: 572 (*Werke* 23: 597).

121. *TSV* 2: 493. The exclusion of landowners from the analysis of capitalism and the utilization of a two-class model is theoretically defended at *TSV* 2: 152.

122. This belief is vigorously expressed by the *Communist Manifesto* (see *SW* 1: 109), but Marx seems to have had doubts about it later. *TSV* 2: 573; *TSV* 3: 63.

123. *SW* 1: 116.

124. *Poverty*, p. 173.

125. See "Contribution to the Critique of Hegel's Philosophy of Law. Introduction," in *Collected Works* 3: 183–87.

126. *SW* 1: 478–79. On the issue of peasant class consciousness, see Mayer, pp. 148–49, 108–9.

127. *SW* 2: 291; see also Marx's letter to Bolte, November 23, 1871.

128. Poulantzas, *Political Power*, pp. 63–64; also p. 66.

129. *Ibid.*, p. 70n.

Chapter Two

1. *Cap.* 1: 372n.

2. *Poverty*, p. 122; from the same period, see Marx to Annenkov, December 28, 1846, quoted at p. 162 above.

3. *SW* 1: 62 (*Werke* 3: 73).

4. *SW* 1: 70 (*Werke* 3: 72).

5. See *SW* 1: 519, 534 n.6.

6. *Cap.* 3: 883–84 (*Werke* 25: 891); also p. 878 (885).

7. *SW* 1: 160, emphasis omitted.

8. *TSV* 3: 430.

9. See *SW* 1: 62.

10. For example, Engels to C. Schmidt, August 5 and October 27, 1890 (in *SW* 3).

11. *SW* 1: 19–20, 30 (*Werke* 3: 20–21, 28).

12. *SW* 3: 162.

13. *SW* 1: 518–19; *Poverty*, p. 122.

14. *SW* 2: 387; *SW* 1: 37, 64; *Werke* 4: 338–39; see *TSV* 2: 580; on capitalism's preparation for socialism, see *Grundrisse*, pp. 325, 707 (Dietz, pp. 231, 594–95). This, by the way, suggests a historical materialist explanation of social stratification in the U.S.S.R.

15. *SW* 1: 518.

16. Plekhanov, *Fundamental Problems*, pp. 49–50; *Monist View of History*, pp. 129–31, 216–17. At the last place cited Plekhanov writes: "The development of the productive forces is itself determined by the qualities of the geographical environment surrounding man."

17. For example, *Cap.* 1: 512–14 (*Werke* 23: 535–37); *SW* 1: 20.

18. Federn, pp. 14, 16.

19. Marx to Annenkov, *SW* 1: 522; see Pannekoek, p. 18; Stalin, pp. 29ff.

20. See Engels to Schmidt, August 5, 1890; to Block, September 21–22, 1890; to Schmidt, October 27, 1890; to Mehring, July 14, 1893; to Borgius (Starkenburg), January 25, 1894 (all available in *SW* 3).

21. *Cap.* 1: 82n (*Werke* 23: 96n), my emphasis.

22. Benedetto Croce seems to hold something like the position criticized here, in his belief that no cause or group of causes leads from one socioeconomic form to another in general because the causes and circumstances differ in each case (Croce, pp. 91–92). Croce would have saluted the consequence that historical materialism could be no science; for him it was only an aid to understanding history. Neither science nor philosophy of history, historical materialism simply emphasizes some previously neglected (i.e., economic) aspects of history. Even if Croce were correct about this, he could hardly have thought that the intentions of the founders of historical materialism were so modest.

23. Addis, "Freedom and the Marxist Philosophy of History," p. 155; see McMurtry, pp. 254–61.

24. *Cap.* 1: 18 (*Werke* 23: 26); *Grundrisse*, pp. 85–88 (Dietz, pp. 6–10); see Marx to Annenkov, *SW* 1: 522, on "economic categories."

25. Engels to Schmidt, August 5, 1890 (my emphasis). Engels continues: "Up to now but little has been done because only a few people have got down to it seriously."

26. But see Leonard Krieger's stimulating essay, which argues that

Engels' problems in specifying the base-superstructure connection led him in effect to do just this—to affirm empirical historiography at the expense of theory. "Editor's Introduction" to Engels, *The German Revolutions*. Also see Gareth Stedman Jones, "Engels and the End of Classical German Philosophy."

27. Plekhanov, *Fundamental Problems*, pp. 108–10, 139–40; Labriola, pp. 140–55.

28. Engels, *Dialectics of Nature*, p. 174. The inadequacy of ancient Greek dialectical thought was precisely its inability to dissect and analyze nature—its inability to master the separate phenomena. *SW* 3: 62–63; *Anti-Dühring*, p. 27.

29. Ollman, *Alienation*, e.g., pp. 17–19, 29–30; Charles Evans, pp. 184–85, 186. See Davidson, p. 54: "The truth of a causal statement depends on *what* events are described; its status as analytic or synthetic depends on *how* the events are described."

30. MacIver, p. 412.

31. Witt-Hansen, Chapter III, section C.

32. An unpublished manuscript by G. A. Cohen helped me to clarify this and the following paragraph.

33. See Marx to Annenkov (*SW* 1: 519): "With the acquisition of new productive faculties, men change their mode of production [in the narrow sense—WHS] and with the mode of production all the economic relations which are merely the necessary relations of this particular mode of production."

34. *SW* 1: 40.

Chapter Three

1. "Conceptually, *competition* is nothing other than the inner *nature of capital*." *Grundrisse*, p. 414 (Dietz, p. 317). Although I am concerned in this first section with the perspective of Volume One of *Das Kapital*, I do draw on Marx's other economic writings—but only insofar as they illuminate positions taken in *Capital* I.

2. *Cap.* 1: 613.

3. *Cap.* 1: 619. Elsewhere, Marx says that it is a fairy tale to hold that with the accumulation of capital, the demand for labor could be *constantly* greater than its supply, thus continually raising real wages and lowering the rate of profit. *TSV* 2: 438.

4. *Cap.* 1: 621. This was, of course, recognized before Marx, who reminds his reader that "Ricardo elaborated the point that bourgeois production is not production of wealth for the *producers*." *TSV* 3: 55.

5. *Cap.* 1: 309. Capitalism's "boundless thirst for surplus-labor" contrasts with all other economic formations. *Ibid.*, p. 235.

6. The historical role of capitalism and its necessity for socialism is a constant theme of Marx, but it is put in a particularly striking fashion at *TSV* 2: 118.

7. *Cap.* 1: 627 (*Werke* 23: 656).

8. *Cap.* 3: 222, 249; *TSV* 2: 492; *Cap.* 1: 645.

9. *Cap.* 1: 632.

10. *Cap.* 1: 632–33; see *TSV* 2: 583.

11. *Grundrisse*, p. 399, also pp. 400, 604–5; *TSV* 1: 227; *TSV* 2: 573; *Cap.* 1: 407; *Cap.* 3: 249.

12. *Cap.* 1: 636; *TSV* 2: 477–78; *TSV* 3: 306. In the *Grundrisse* (pp. 400–401), Marx writes: "Hence the tendency of capital simultaneously to increase the *laboring population* as well as to reduce constantly its *necessary* part (constantly to posit a part of it as reserve). And the increase of population itself [is] the chief means for reducing the necessary part."

13. *Cap.* 1: 639–40, 645. Compare the "dogma of the economists," at p. 637.

14. *Cap.* 1: 645.

15. *Ibid.*

16. *Cap.* 1: 644.

17. For further discussion, see Sowell's "Marx's 'Increasing Misery' Doctrine" and Meek's "Marx's 'Doctrine of Increasing Misery'" in his *Economics and Ideology*.

18. *Cap.* 1: 645; see also 646n, 657; *Poverty*, p. 123.

19. *Cap.* 1: 763.

20. *Cap.* 1: 763 (*Werke* 23: 791).

21. In *Socialism: Utopian and Scientific*, Engels identifies this as the fundamental contradiction, "whence arise all the contradictions in which our present-day society moves" (*SW* 3: 150).

22. For example, see Geras, p. 36.

23. *SW* 1: 500–501; see *The German Ideology*, p. 495.

24. For example, Tucker, *Philosophy and Myth*, p. 166, and *The Marxian Revolutionary Idea*, pp. 16–17; Althusser, *For Marx*, p. 99. But see Godelier, "Structure and Contradiction in *Capital*."

25. *Cap.* 3: 220.

26. *Cap.* 3: 232 (Chapter XIV, "Counteracting Influences"). Nonetheless, it is "in every respect the most important law of modern political economy." *Grundrisse*, p. 748 (Dietz, p. 634). The most important counteracting influence is the increase in the intensity of exploitation, which by raising the rate of surplus value offsets a decline in the profit rate. Significantly, however, the same factors which intensify labor also tend to reduce the quantity of labor employed and thus lessen the rate of profit. This connection seems to have been overlooked by both Paul Sweezy and Joan Robinson, who criticize Marx for assuming a constant rate of surplus value. But Marx made no such assumption; see *Cap.* 3: 240. Sweezy, *The Theory of Capitalist Development*, pp. 100–102; Robinson, p. 36.

27. *Cap.* 3: 242.

28. *TSV* 2: 534–35; see *Cap.* 1: 6, 453. Overproduction and market saturation constitute an early (and recurrent) theme in Marx and Engels. For example, *SW* 1: 86–87, 113–14; *The Revolutions of 1848*, pp. 274, 282–85, 297; *Articles on Britain*, pp. 226–27.

29. *Cap.* 3: 244 (*Werke* 25: 254); see *Grundrisse*, pp. 403–4.

30. *Cap.* 1: 356; also, see *TSV* 2: 492; *Cap.* 2: 319; *Grundrisse*, p. 414 (Dietz, p. 317). Engels already understood the unavoidability of disequilibrium and disproportional production under capitalism in his early "Outlines of a Critique of Political Economy" (in *Collected Works* 3), as Marx acknowledged (Marx to Engels, January 8, 1868). Also see Engels' *The Condition of the Working Class*, pp. 114–15.

31. *TSV* 2: 530, 532.

32. See *TSV* 2: 500, 507, 510; *Critique*, p. 96.

33. *TSV* 2: 514.

34. *Cap.* 1: 138; *TSV* 2: 514. The credit system itself exemplifies what will be seen to be the contradictory character of the whole system; see *Cap.* 3: 441.

35. *Cap.* 2: 500, 473. Quesnay's influence on Volume Two has often been noted. Elsewhere, Marx says that John Barton was the first to observe that the component parts of capital do not grow evenly with accumulation and the development of the productive forces. *TSV* 2: 577.

36. *Cap.* 3: 244.

37. *Cap.* 3: 245; see Sweezy, *The Theory of Capitalist Development*, pp. 162–189.

38. *Cap.* 3: 484 (my emphasis). Also, *Cap.* 2: 320n.

39. *TSV* 2: 492, 468. For a misguided attempt to remove the thesis of underconsumption from the corpus of Marxian economics, see Yaffe, esp. pp. 212–14. While Yaffe does this in order to accent the falling rate of profit, Roberts and Stephenson repudiate underconsumption (p. 63) and ignore the thesis of the falling rate of profit in order to stress the primacy of disproportionality in Marx's economic analysis.

40. *Cap.* 2: 415.

41. See *Cap.* 3: 262 (*Werke* 25: 272–73); *Cap.* 1: 392.

42. See *TSV* 3: 122 (*Werke* 26.3: 119).

43. *Cap.* 3: 249.

44. *Cap.* 3: 250 (*Werke* 25: 260).

45. I thank G. A. Cohen for bringing this type of fettering to my attention.

46. See Sweezy, Chapter XI, for a good account of the history of the breakdown theory.

47. Avineri, *Social and Political Thought*. Marx no doubt held this development to be dialectical in some sense, but if Marxian "materialist dialectics" is to be non-idealist, it must mean that the material basis of history—and not its dialectical appearance and forms—provides the explanatory guide. (But see text pp. 107–10.)

48. Avineri, *Social and Political Thought*, pp. 181, 177, 175. See also *Cap.* 3: 436–41.

49. *Cap.* 3: 387; *SW* 2: 16–17. See *Cap.* 1: 331n, for a humorous example offered by Marx.

50. Marx specifically mentions joint-stock companies as a means of centralization at *Cap.* 1: 628.

51. *Cap.* 1: 332.

52. *Cap.* 3: 440; see *Anti-Dühring*, pp. 312–13.

53. *Cap.* 3: 264.

54. *TSV* 3: 426 (*Werke* 26.3, p. 418); a similar passage appears at *Cap.* 3: 266 (*Werke* 25: 276–77).

55. *Cap.* 1: 20 (*Werke* 23: 27–8); see the young Lenin, *Collected Works*, Vol. 1, p. 165ff. On "process," see *Le Capital*, p. 77n.

56. See Chapter Two, footnote on p. 73 and accompanying text.

57. *Cap.* 1: 19 (*Werke* 23: 27).

58. *Anti-Dühring*, p. 152. George Lichtheim, however, claims that Engels' defense "hardly does justice to Marx." *Marxism*, p. 256. One must recall that the *Anti-Dühring* was written with Marx's approval and assistance, and as fussy as Marx was about such matters, it is hard to believe that he would allow Engels to misrepresent his position.

59. *Collected Works* 3: 186 (*Werke* 1: 390, translation modified); see *The Holy Family*, p. 52 (*Werke* 2: 38).

60. *Cap.* 1: 302.

61. See Chapter One, note 122 and accompanying text, as well as the footnote on p. 95 of this chapter and Nicolaus, "Proletariat and Middle Class in Marx."

62. *SW* 1: 501; see also *TSV* 3: 315.

63. See *SW* 2: 17, 19.

64. For example, *SW* 2: 293; *Articles on Britain*, p. 119 ("The Chartists"); *Cap.* 1: 6; see Hook, pp. 290–97, and R. Landor, "Interview with Karl Marx."

65. *SW* 3: 15.

66. See *The German Ideology* (p. 487): "In reality, of course, what happened was that people won freedom for themselves each time to the extent that was dictated and permitted not by their ideal of man, but by the existing productive forces." Lichtheim misses this point; see his discussion of the "heart of Marxism," *Marxism*, p. 238.

67. For example, Rubel, p. 196.

68. *Cap.* 1: 653.

69. *Cap.* 1: 487; *TSV* 3: 444. (For a somewhat different assessment of this passage, see Braverman, p. 231n.) Marx claims the historic tendency of capitalist production, as presented in *Capital*, is to create "the elements of a new economic order, by giving the greatest impulse at once to the productive forces of social labor and *to the integral development of every individual producer*" (letter to the Editor of *Notes on the Fatherland*, November 1877; my emphasis). Despite the contradictory form of this tendency, it would appear that the laborer is less "a crippled monstrosity" under modern industry than under manufacture; see *Cap.* 1: 360.

70. *Cap.* 1: 737.

71. *Articles on Britain*, p. 192; see p. 224; Engels to Marx, September 24, 1852; and see the excerpts from their letters given in *Selected Correspondence*, London 1936, pp. 85–86. Crash and crisis, however, seem to

give way to chronic slump in Engels' later reflections—a historical development which seems less likely to galvanize the working class into revolutionary activity. See *Cap.* 1: 6, and *Articles on Britain*, pp. 392–93.

72. Marx to J. Weydemeyer, March 5, 1852.

Chapter Four

1. *Anti-Dühring*, p. 171.

2. Morgan, *Ancient Society* (hereafter, *AS*); Marx's 98 pages of manuscript notes on Morgan are available in *The Ethnological Notebooks of Karl Marx (EN)*. According to Engels, Marx wished to present Morgan's results along with some conclusions of his own to the German public. *SW* 3: 191; Engels to Kautsky, February 16, 1884.

3. *Cap.* 1: 178. Early man was the child of nature, not its master (see *Cap.* 1: 513), but it is rather misleading to suggest, as Anthony Giddens does, that as a result primitive man was "alienated." Giddens, *Class Structure*, p. 26, and *Capitalism*, pp. 219, 220.

4. *PCEF*, pp. 69, 90–91 (Dietz, pp. 376, 392); *Cap.* 3: 831. Tribalism is the basis of primordial existence; see *Peasant War*, p. 136.

5. *Cap.* 1: 79; see p. 334, *SW* 3: 267. Although these ties are limiting and one-sided in the development which they afford the individual, they are satisfying and agreeable to him, and it would be philistine, notes Marx, to see the primitive bonds of the group as despotic. *EN*: 326, 329; see *SW* 1: 492.

6. *Cap.* 1: 77; *Grundrisse*, p. 88.

7. *PCEF*, p. 82 (Dietz, pp. 385–86).

8. *Cap.* 1: 77–78n (quoting Marx's *Critique of Political Economy*, p. 33n).

9. Consider for example, Marx's description of early Roumania at *Cap.* 1: 237.

10. *PCEF*, p. 95 (Dietz, p. 395).

11. *Cap.* 1: 351.

12. Marx and Engels, *The Russian Menace to Europe*, p. 223. Reference is to the second draft of Marx's March 8, 1881 letter to V. Zasulich, selections from the three drafts of which are presented there. Hobsbawm offers a brief portion of two of the drafts in *PCEF*, and *SW* 1 contains the entire first draft. Originally published in Russian by Ryazanoff in the first volume of *Arkhiv Marksa i Engel'sa*, a full German version of the three preliminary drafts—written by Marx in French—is available in *Werke* 19.

13. *PCEF*, p. 144.

14. See Engels' "The Mark" in *The Peasant War in Germany* or Marx's draft letters to Zasulich.

15. *PCEF*, p. 145.

16. *SW* 1: 21–22; *EN*, p. 133; *AS*, p. 540. Marx and Engels still stressed that the family mirrored the antagonisms of the society around it. *SW* 3: 234; *EN*, p. 120; see *AS*, p. 491.

17. *PCEF*, p. 89. Population pressure may play a part in this; see pp. 92–93 and *Articles on Britain*, pp. 163–64.

18. *PCEF*, p. 91 (Dietz, p. 392).

19. *PCEF*, p. 95 (Dietz, p. 395); see *The German Ideology*, p. 170.

20. *SW* 3: 231; *Anti-Dühring*, pp. 205–7.

21. *SW* 3: 317, 319.

22. *SW* 1: 22.

23. *Cap.* 1: 87, 351–52; see *Critique*, p. 50; *Grundrisse*, pp. 740, 882, 103; *Cap.* 3: 177; *Anti-Dühring*, p. 184.

24. *SW* 2: 393; *Anti-Dühring*, p. 184; see Plekhanov, *Monist View of History*, p. 169.

25. *SW* 3: 324. Morgan refers to private property as a passion which dominates all others, and Engels stresses the role of greed in dividing the members of the gentes. *AS*, pp. 6, 540; *SW* 3: 322, 333, 267. Perhaps this passion was stimulated by a shortage of land (see *SW* 3: 76).

26. *Cap.* 3: 616; see *Grundrisse*, p. 246.

27. *PCEF*, p. 93; see *SW* 3: 324, where Engels says: "Just as hetaerism and prostitution clung to the heels of monogamy, so from now on mortgage clung to the ownership of land."

28. *Cap.* 3: 806; *Cap.* 1: 334n.

29. *EN*, p. 210.

30. *Ibid.*; *Grundrisse*, p. 540.

31. *EN*, p. 213; *SW* 3: 322. By contrast, production among the Iroquois had not developed sufficiently to give rise to social antagonism. *SW* 3: 278.

32. *SW* 3: 326, 330.

33. *Cap.* 2: 119–20, 483; *Cap.* 3: 786–87; see Maurice Dobb, *Studies in the Development of Capitalism*, pp. 6–8.

34. *SW* 3: 484. Still, the *Anti-Dühring* (p. 172) credits Marx's researches with yielding "all that has up to now been established on the theory of pre-bourgeois economy."

35. See Wittfogel, pp. 372–415; Varga, "The Asiatic Mode of Production" in his *Politico-Economic Problems of Capitalism*; Eberhard, pp. 66–74; D'Encausse and Schram, pp. 7–9, 92–97.

36. For example, Lichtheim, "Marx and the Asiatic Mode of Production"; Thorner, "Marx on India and the Asiatic Mode of Production"; and Anderson's recent *Lineages of the Absolutist State*, esp. pp. 473–83. For a discussion of the intellectual antecedents of Marx's concept of the Asiatic mode of production, see pp. 462–72, there, or (more briefly) Lowe, *The Function of "China" in Marx, Lenin, and Mao*, pp. 1–6.

37. Marx to Engels, June 14, 1853; on the Asian contrast of social immobility and restless political activity, see *Werke* 15: 514.

38. *PCEF*, pp. 69–70. Balibar, pp. 218–19 in Althusser and Balibar, makes an interesting comparison of this with the "fetishism" which occurs according to Marx under capitalism.

39. *PCEF*, pp. 70, 83; see *Cap.* 3: 333–34.

40. Marx to Engels, March 14, 1868 (quoted at *PCEF*, p. 139); see *TSV* 3: 422–23; *PCEF*, p. 67.

41. *Grundrisse*, p. 882.

42. *SW* 1: 108–9n; *Anti-Dühring*, p. 200.

43. Thorner, p. 60; *Cap.* 1: 334n (*Werke* 23: 354n), my emphasis.

44. *Cap.* 1: 357–58 (*Werke* 23: 378–79).

45. *Cap.* 1: 339–40; *SW* 1: 43; see also *EN*, p. 183, and Krader, pp. 245–46.

46. Thorner, p. 66.

47. *SW* 1: 489, 491; *Anti-Dühring*, p. 205; *PCEF*, pp. 70–71; see Plekhanov, *Fundamental Problems of Marxism*, p. 117.

48. For example, *Marx on China* pp. 2, 56.

49. *TSV* 3: 435; Marx to Engels, June 2, 1853; *Grundrisse*, p. 467; *PCEF*, pp. 77–78.

50. Richard Jones, as quoted by Marx at *Cap.* 1: 333.

51. Marx says that the productive forces of India are paralyzed by lack of exchange and transport. *SW* 1: 495–96; *Grundrisse*, p. 525; *PCEF*, p. 143.

52. *TSV* 1: 277; Godelier, "La Notion de 'Mode de Production Asiatique'," p. 65; Chesneaux, pp. 44–45.

53. The quotation is from *Cap.* 1: 514, note 2; see *Anti-Dühring*, p. 205. The fading of this explanation peeves Karl Wittfogel; see his catalogue of Marx's backslidings, *Oriental Despotism*, pp. 381–82. Lawrence Krader suggests that the old Marx followed Maine in assigning little importance to the great works of the Orient in understanding Asian society, but the evidence for this is less than conclusive; see Krader's "Introduction," *EN*, p. 39.

54. *Cap.* 3: 791, 634; see *EN*, pp. 281, 282; on the collective responsibility of the community for taxes to the state, see Marx to Engels, November 7, 1868.

55. *Cap.* 3: 791.

56. Compare Hegel, p. 105.

57. *Cap.* 1: 82n.

58. March 8, 1855. Debt relations played a key role in this struggle; see *Cap.* 1: 135–36.

59. *Cap.* 3: 595, 598–99; *Grundrisse*, p. 806; *Cap.* 1:726–27n. See pp. 121–23 above.

60. *Cap.* 1: 334n.

61. *Anti-Dühring*, p. 206.   62. *Grundrisse*, p. 107.

63. *TSV* 2: 502–3.   64. *TSV* 2: 528.

65. *Cap.* 2: 483; *Articles on Britain*, p. 163; see *PCEF*, p. 92–93; Weber, pp. 78–79. The slaves themselves continually died out. *SW* 1: 72.

66. *SW* 3: 308–9.

67. J. E. Cairnes, as quoted by Marx at *Cap.* 1: 266.

68. *Cap.* 1: 196n.

69. *Cap.* 3: 384; "Resultate," pp. 78–8on, 118 (ms. pp. 469k, 477).

70. *TSV* 1: 301; see *SW* 3: 310, 284.

71. *SW* 1: 108.

72. *SW* 3: 315. Engels contrasts this with "the serfs of the Middle Ages [who], step by step, achieved their emancipation as a class."

73. *SW* 1: 395.

74. Marx discusses the failure of capitalism to develop in Rome with regard both to the initial dissolution of peasant proprietorship (letter to the Editor of *Notes on the Fatherland*, November 1877) and to the extinction of the ancient mode of production proper (*PCEF*, pp. 109–10).

75. *SW* 1: 108–9.

76. Marx to Engels, February 27, 1861; see *Werke* 31: 598. Actually, Marx refers to him not as a slave, but as a "real representative of the ancient proletariat," but presumably this was an honorific.

77. Zhukov, p. 78; Mashkin, "The Workers' Revolution."

78. *SW* 3: 284. Engels argues that they were able to pull down the state because they were the majority of the free population—although by his own estimate the patricians had at their command slaves numbering three times the total of free men.

79. *SW* 3: 308; see Marx at *SW* 3: 159.

80. *SW* 3: 311; *Cap.* 1: 724; see *Cap.* 3: 900.

81. *SW* 1: 22.

82. *SW* 3: 311–14; *Peasant War*, pp. 145–46.

83. On Charlemagne's military service, see *Cap.* 1: 727n; *Cap.* 3: 599; *SW* 3: 312. On corvée labor in Roumania, see *Cap.* 1: 237.

84. *Grundrisse*, p. 98 (Dietz, p. 19).

85. *SW* 1: 71; *Grundrisse*, p. 97 (Dietz, p. 18).

86. Engels to Marx, December 16, 1882.

87. *SW* 1: 23.

88. Engels to Marx, December 22, 1882. Years before, in reference to another example, Marx had written to Engels (October 30, 1856) that "here serfdom can be shown to have arisen in a purely economic way, without the intermediate link of conquest and racial dualism."

89. *SW* 1: 72 (*Werke* 3: 64); but see *Grundrisse*, p. 97.

90. For example, Dobb, *Studies*, pp. 35–37; Kosminsky, pp. vi–vii. But see Paul Sweezy in Sweezy, Dobb, et al.; Anderson, *Lineages*, pp. 17, 402–3.

91. *Cap.* 1: 77.

92. *Grundrisse*, p. 650.

93. *Cap.* 1: 750; see *SW* 1: 53, 67, 109.

94. *SW* 1: 23.

95. See *SW* 1, p. 72: "Rome indeed never became more than a city; its connection with the provinces was almost exclusively political and could, therefore, easily be broken again by political events."

96. See "Resultate," p. 174; *TSV* 1: 389; *Cap.* 3: 878. This point is

missed by Leff, p. 148; (Althusser and) Balibar, pp. 303–4 and *passim*; and Plamenatz, *Man and Society*, II, pp. 282–83. This error is the basis of Althusser and Balibar's denial—supposedly on Marx's behalf—of both the claim that capitalist production relations arose in response to the development of the productive forces and the general determination of the relations of production by the productive forces.

97. *SW* 1: 113; see *The Poverty of Philosophy*, p. 122.

98. *Cap.* 1: 715 (*Werke* 23: 743).

99. *Cap.* 1: 715–16. *The German Ideology* (p. 382) refers to "the epoch *between* the rule of the aristocracy and the rule of the bourgeoisie" (my emphasis).

100. *Reading Capital*, pp. 282–83; See *Cap.* 1: 248, 310; *PCEF*, pp. 111–12.

101. Letter to the Editor of *Notes on the Fatherland*, November 1877.

102. *Cap.* 1: 716.

103. *Cap.* 1: 334n, 718n (*Werke* 23: 354n, 745n); but see *The Revolutions of 1848*, p. 249.

104. *Cap.* 1: 761; see *Cap.* 3: 807.

105. *Cap.* 1: 762; *SW* 3: 152.

106. *Peasant War*, p. 178.

107. *Cap.* 3: 794.   108. *Cap.* 3: 797–98.

109. *PCEF*, p. 105.   110. *Cap.* 3: 807.

111. *SW* 1: 66–67.

112. Marx to Engels, July 27, 1854; see *SW* 1: 110; *Poverty*, p. 173. Avineri rather expansively extrapolates from this letter to support his view that capitalism results from the creation of "a civil society," which is the product of the medieval communal movement. Avineri, *Karl Marx*, pp. 154–55. Compare Marx on the wane of the sovereign towns, text at note 99, p. 139, above.

113. *PCEF*, p. 118; "Resultate," p. 110 (ms. p. 475).

114. See *SW* 1: 54, 519. "The urban labor of the Middle Ages already constitutes a great advance and serves as a preparatory school for the capitalist mode of production, as regards the continuity and steadiness of labor." *TSV* 3: 434.

115. *PCEF*, p. 112; see "Resultate," pp. 106–8.

116. *Cap.* 1: 761–62.

117. *Cap.* 1: 308–9; "Resultate," p. 110; *Poverty*, p. 38.

118. *Cap.* 1: 335, 624.

119. *Cap.* 1: 762.

120. *Cap.* 1: 760; cf. *SW* 1: 109–13.

121. *Cap.* 1: 751.

122. *Cap.* 1: 750; on usury, see *Cap.* 3: 593–94, 597, 610; for its effect on feudalism, see *Grundrisse*, pp. 836, 854; *TSV* 3: pp. 530–32; *Cap.* 1: 135–36.

123. *Cap.* 3: 327; see pp. 325–333 *passim*; also *Cap.* 1: 510, *PCEF*, p. 112.

124. *Peasant War*, p. 180. Along this line, *Cap.* 1: 146n, contrasts "the power, based on the personal relations of dominion and servitude, that is conferred by landed property, and the impersonal power that is given by money."

125. *PCEF*, p. 115.

126. *TSV* 3: 469; Marx to Engels, April 2, 1858: "Real capital arises from that money, or merchants' capital, which gains control of production."

127. *Cap.* 3: 334.

128. *Cap.* 1: 308, 332; "Resultate," p. 94 (ms. p. 471).

129. "Resultate," p. 112 (ms. p. 476).

130. *Cap.* 1: 750. On the social background of these incipient capitalists, see also *Grundrisse*, p. 468.

131. *Grundrisse*, pp. 893, 641 (Dietz, pp. 853, 535). "Like any other specific mode of production, [capitalism] presupposes a given level of the social productive forces." *Cap.* 3: 878.

132. "Resultate," p. 184 (ms. p. 442).

Chapter Five

1. See *SW* 3: 155–56.

2. *The Holy Family*, p. 51 (*Werke* 2: 37).

3. *Grundrisse*, p. 749 (Dietz, p. 635), translation modified and emphasis added.

4. For example, *Grundrisse*, pp. 540, 605 (Deitz, pp. 438–39, 498); *Cap.* 1: 235, 486.

5. In his "Karl Marx's Philosophy of History," D. R. Gandy argues that the "Preface" model was intended by Marx to apply only to capitalism. This is clearly false, although one can understand why Gandy wishes it to be true.

6. See Croce, p. 90.

7. *Grundrisse*, p. 193 (Dietz, p. 108).

8. Marxists Paul Baran and Eric Hobsbawm ("Stages of Economic Growth," p. 240) acknowledge this: "No bloodless schema of 5 (or 3 or 7) 'stages' can do justice to the multitude and variety of economic, technological, and ideological configurations generated by this never-ceasing battle between the forces and relations of production."

9. For example, Hicks' *A Theory of Economic History* (1969). Marx, however, would have thought that Hicks does not give the productive forces their due.

10. *Grundrisse*, p. 158 (Dietz, p. 75).

11. This list was suggested to me by G. A. Cohen who, in an unpublished manuscript, correlates these stages with the following levels of productive development: no surplus, some surplus, moderately high surplus, massive surplus.

12. *SW* 1: 522 (letter to Annenkov).

13. See Harré, esp. Chapters 4 and 5.

14. This paragraph draws on the ideas of the late Imre Lakatos (with a tip of the hat to Paul Feyerabend), although I do not attempt to do them justice here. See Lakatos, "Falsification and the Methodology of Scientific Research Programmes," and Feyerabend, "Against Method."

15. Lakatos, p. 119; in the original, the sentence is italicized.

16. The provisional nature of scientific progress is not something which has been well appreciated by Marx's followers who, as Lauer points out, tend to equate "knowledge," "apodictic verification," and "that which is scientifically established." Such a notion implies that the "truths" of the Marxist classics are incorrigible—that science never goes back to criticize what it has already established. See Lauer, "The Marxist Conception of Science."

Bibliography

Acton, Harry B. *The Illusion of the Epoch*. Boston, 1957.
———. *What Marx Really Said*. London, 1967.
Addis, Laird. "Freedom and the Marxist Philosophy of History." *Philosophy of Science*, Vol. 33, Nos. 1–2, March–June 1966.
———. *The Logic of Society*. Minneapolis, 1975.
Althusser, Louis. *For Marx*. New York, 1970.
———. *Lenin and Philosophy and Other Essays*. London, 1971.
———. *Politics and History*. London, 1972.
Althusser, Louis, and Etienne Balibar. *Reading Capital*. London, 1970.
Anderson, Perry. *Lineages of the Absolutist State*. London, 1974.
———. *Passages from Antiquity to Feudalism*. London, 1974.
Arthur, John. "Systemic Explanation and Marxian Methodology," Ph.D. diss. (philosophy), Vanderbilt Univ., 1973.
Avineri, Shlomo, ed. *Marx's Socialism*. New York, 1973.
———. *The Social and Political Thought of Karl Marx*. Cambridge, 1971.
Baran, Paul, and Eric Hobsbawm. "Stages of Economic Growth." *Kylos*, Vol. 14, No. 2, 1961.
Blackburn, Robin, ed. *Ideology in Social Science*. Bungay (Suffolk), 1972.
Bober, Mandell M. *Karl Marx's Interpretation of History*. 2d ed. New York, 1965.
Boudin, Louis B. *The Theoretical System of Karl Marx*. Chicago, 1918.
Braverman, Harry. *Labor and Monopoly Capital*. New York, 1974.
Brewster, Ben. "Introduction to Lukács on Bukharin." *New Left Review* 39, September–October 1966.
Bukharin, Nikolai. *Historical Materialism*. Ann Arbor, 1969.
Chesneaux, Jean. "Où en est la Discussion sur le Mode de Production Asiatique?" *La Pensée*, No. 129, October 1966.
Cohen, G. A. "Karl Marx and the Withering Away of Social Science." *Philosophy and Public Affairs*, Vol. 1, No. 2, Winter 1972.

———. "Marx's Dialectic of Labor." *Philosophy and Public Affairs*, Vol. 3, No. 3, Spring 1974.

Cohen, G. A., and H. B. Acton. "On Some Criticisms of Historical Materialism" (symposium). *Aristotelian Society, Proceedings*, 1970 Supplement.

Colletti, Lucio. *From Rousseau to Lenin*. London, 1972.

———. *Marxism and Hegel*. London, 1973.

Cornforth, Maurice. *Dialectical Materialism. Vol. 2, Historical Materialism*. London, 1953.

Croce, Benedetto. *Historical Materialism and the Economics of Karl Marx*. London, 1966.

Dahrendorf, Ralf. *Class and Class Conflict in Industrial Society*. Stanford, 1959.

Davidson, Donald. "Actions, Reasons, and Causes." In May Brodbeck, ed., *Readings in the Philosophy of the Social Sciences*. New York, 1968.

D'Encausse, H. Carrère, and Stuart Schram, eds. *Marxism and Asia*. London, 1969.

Dobb, Maurice. *Studies in the Development of Capitalism*. London, 1963.

———. "The Transition from Feudalism to Capitalism." In B. Singh and V. B. Singh, eds., *Social and Economic Change*. Calcutta, 1967.

Draper, Hal. "Marx and the Dictatorship of the Proletariat." *Cahiers de L'I.S.E.A.*, September 1962 (Series S, *Études de Marxologie* 6).

———. "Marx on Democratic Forms of Government." In Ralph Miliband and John Saville, eds., *The Socialist Register 1974*. London.

Eberhard, Wolfram. *Conquerors and Rulers*. Leiden, 1965.

Engels, Frederick. *The Condition of the Working Class in England*. London, 1969.

———. *Dialectics of Nature*. Translated by Clemens Dutt. London, 1941.

———. *Herr Eugen Dühring's Revolution in Science [Anti-Dühring]*. Translated by Emile Burns. Moscow and Leningrad, 1934.

———. *The Peasant War in Germany*. Moscow, 1965.

Evans, Charles. "A New Philosophical Interpretation of Marx." *Social Research*, Vol. 40, No. 1, Spring 1973.

Evans, Michael. *Karl Marx*. London, 1975.

Federn, Karl. *The Materalist Conception of History*. London, 1939.

Feyerabend, Paul. "Against Method." In Michael Radner and Stephen Winokur, eds., *Minnesota Studies for the Philosophy of Science 4*. Minneapolis, 1970.

Gandy, Daniel R. "Karl Marx's Philosophy of History: A New Interpretation." Ph.D. diss. (philosophy), Univ. of Texas, 1967.

Gellner, Ernest. "The Soviet and the Savage." *Times Literary Supplement* (London), October 18, 1974.

General Council of the First International, The. Five volumes. Moscow, n.d.

Geras, Norman. "Rosa Luxemburg: Barbarism and the Collapse of Capitalism." *New Left Review* 82, November–December 1973.

Giddens, Anthony. *Capitalism and Modern Social Theory*. Cambridge, 1971.

————. *The Class Structure of the Advanced Societies*. London, 1973.

Godelier, Maurice. "La Notion de 'Mode de Production Asiatique' et Les Schémas Marxistes d'Evolution des Sociétés." In Centre d'Études et de Recherches Marxistes, *Sur le "Mode de Production Asiatique."* Paris, 1969.

————. *Rationality and Irrationality in Economics*. London, 1972.

————. "Structure and Contradiction in *Capital*." In Robin Blackburn, ed., *Ideology in Social Science*.

Gough, Ian. "Productive and Unproductive Labour in Marx." *New Left Review* 76, November–December 1972.

Harré, R. *The Philosophies of Science*. Oxford, 1972.

Harris, Abram L. "Pure Capitalism and the Disappearance of the Middle Class." *Journal of Political Economy*, Vol. 47, No. 3, June 1939.

Hegel, Georg W. F. *The Philosophy of History*. New York, 1956.

Heilbroner, Robert L. *Between Capitalism and Socialism*. New York, 1970.

Hicks, John. *A Theory of Economic History*. Oxford, 1969.

Hindess, Barry, and Paul Q. Hirst. *Pre-Capitalist Modes of Production*. London, 1975.

Hodgson, Geoff. "The Theory of the Falling Rate of Profit." *New Left Review* 84, March–April 1974.

Hoffmann, Ernst. "Social Economic Formations and Historical Science." *Marxism Today*, September 1965.

Hook, Sidney. *Towards the Understanding of Karl Marx*. New York, 1933.

Horowitz, David, ed. *Marx and Modern Economics*. London, 1968.

Hunt, E. K., and Jesse G. Schwartz, eds. *A Critique of Economic Theory*. Harmondsworth, 1972.

Jones, Gareth Stedman. "Engels and the End of Classical German Philosophy." *New Left Review* 79, May–June 1973.

————. "The Marxism of the Early Lukács: An Evaluation." *New Left Review* 70, November–December 1971.

Korsch, Karl. *Karl Marx*. London, 1938. Reprinted, New York, 1963.

Kosminsky, E. A. *Studies in the Agrarian History of England in the Thirteenth Century*. Oxford, 1956.

Krader, Lawrence. "The Works of Marx and Engels in Ethnology Compared." *International Review of Social History*, Vol. 18, Part 2, 1973.

Krieger, Leonard. "Editor's Introduction" in Friedrich Engels, *The German Revolution*. Chicago, 1967.

————. "Marx and Engels as Historians." *Journal of the History of Ideas*, Vol. 14, No. 381, June 1953.

Labriola, Antonio. *Essays on the Materialistic Conception of History*. New York, 1966.

Lakatos, Imre. "Falsification and the Methodology of Scientific Research Programmes." In Imre Lakatos and Alan Musgrave, eds., *Criticism and the Growth of Knowledge*. Cambridge, 1970.

Landor, R. "The Curtain Raised: Interview with Karl Marx." *New York*

World, July 18, 1871. Reprinted in *The Massachusetts Review*, Vol. 12, No. 3, Summer 1971.

Lange, Oskar. *Political Economy*. Vol. 1, New York, 1963.

Lauer, Quentin. "The Marxist Conception of Science." In R. S. Cohen and M. W. Wartofsky, eds., *Boston Studies in the Philosophy of Science*, Vol. 14. Boston, 1974.

Leff, Gordon. *The Tyranny of Concepts*. 2d ed. London, 1969.

Lenin, V. I. *Collected Works*. Vol. 1, Moscow, 1963.

Lichtheim, George. "Marx and the 'Asiatic Mode of Production'." *St. Anthony's Papers* 14, 1963. Reprinted in Shlomo Avineri, ed., *Marx's Socialism*.

———. *Marxism: An Historical and Critical Study*. London, 1963.

Lowe, Donald M. *The Function of "China" in Marx, Lenin, and Mao*. Berkeley and Los Angeles, 1966.

Lukács, Georg. *History and Class Consciousness*. London, 1971.

———. *Political Writings, 1919–20*. London, 1972.

MacIver, A. M. "Historical Explanation." In Anthony Flew, ed., *Logic and Language* (first and second series). Garden City, N.Y., 1965.

McLellan, David. *Karl Marx: His Life and Thought*. New York, 1973.

McMurtry, John. "Making Sense of Economic Determinism." *Canadian Journal of Philosophy*, Vol. 3, No. 2, December 1973.

Mahov, A. S., and A. S. Frish, eds. *Society and Economic Relations*. Moscow, 1969.

Mandel, Ernest. *The Formation of the Economic Thought of Karl Marx*. London, 1971.

Marx, Karl. *Capital*, Vol. 1. Translated by Samuel Moore and Edward Aveling. London, 1970.

———. *Capital*, Vols. 2 and 3. Moscow, 1967, 1971.

———. *Le Capital*. Translated by Joseph Roy. Paris, n.d. [1875?].

———. *A Contribution to the Critique of Political Economy*. Translated by S. W. Ryazanskaya. London, 1971.

———. *The Ethnological Notebooks of Karl Marx*. Edited with an Introduction by Lawrence Krader. Assen (The Netherlands), 1972.

———. *Grundrisse*. Translated with a Foreword by Martin Nicolaus. Harmondsworth, 1973. Penguin edition.

———. *Grundrisse der Kritik der Politischen Ökonomie*. Berlin, 1953. Dietz Verlag edition.

———. *Marx on China*. Edited by Dona Torr. London, 1968.

———. *Misère de la Philosophie*. Paris, 1908.

———. *The Poverty of Philosophy*. New York, 1963.

———. *Pre-Capitalist Economic Formations*. Edited with an Introduction by Eric Hobsbawm. Translated by Jack Cohen. London, 1964.

———. "*Resultate des Unmittelbaren Produktionsprozesses*." *Arkhiv Marksa i Engel'sa*, Tom II (vii). Moscow, 1933.

———. *The Revolutions of 1848*. Edited with an Introduction by David Fernbach. Harmondsworth, 1973.

———. *Theories of Surplus Value*, Vol. 1. Translated by Emile Burns. Moscow, 1969.

———. *Theories of Surplus Value*, Vol. 2. Translated by Renate Simpson. Moscow, 1968.

———. *Theories of Surplus Value*, Vol. 3. Translated by Jack Cohen. London, 1972.

Marx, Karl, and Frederick Engels. *Articles on Britain*. Moscow, 1971.

———. *Collected Works*, Vols. 1–6. New York, 1975—. (International Publishers; fifty vols. planned.)

———. *The German Ideology* (complete text). Translated by Clemens Dutt (and others). Moscow, 1968.

———. *The Holy Family*. Translated by Richard Dixon. Moscow, 1956.

———. *Letters to Americans*. New York, 1953.

———. *On the Paris Commune*. Moscow, 1971.

———. *The Russian Menace to Europe*. Edited by Paul W. Blackstock and Bert F. Hoselitz. London, 1953.

———. *Selected Correspondence*. Translated by Dona Torr. London, 1936.

———. *Selected Correspondence*. Translated by I. Lasker. Moscow, 1965.

———. *Selected Works*. Three volumes. Moscow, 1969 and 1970.

———. *Werke*. Thirty-nine volumes, with two supplementary volumes. Berlin, 1956–68.

Mashkin, Nickolai A. "The Workers' Revolution and the Fall of the Western Roman Empire." *Journal of General Education*, Vol. 5, No. 1, October 1950.

Mayer, Henry. "Marx, Engels, and the Politics of the Peasantry." *Cahiers de L'I.S.E.A.*, No. 102, June 1960 (Series S, *Études de Marxologie* 3).

Meek, Ronald L. *Economics and Ideology and Other Essays*. London, 1967.

Mill, John Stuart. *Principles of Political Economy*. Harmondsworth, 1970.

Morgan, Lewis Henry. *Ancient Society*. London, 1877.

Nagel, Ernest, ed. *John Stuart Mill's Philosophy of Scientific Method*. New York, 1950.

Nell, Edward J. "Economic Relationships in the Decline of Feudalism: An Examination of Economic Interdependence and Social Change." *History and Theory*, Vol. 6, No. 3, 1967.

Nicolaus, Martin. "Proletariat and Middle Class in Marx: Hegelian Choreography and the Capitalist Dialectic." *Studies on the Left*, Vol. 7, No. 1, January–February 1967.

Ollman, Bertell. *Alienation: Marx's Conception of Man in Capitalist Society*. Cambridge, 1971.

———. "Marx's Use of Class." *American Journal of Sociology*, Vol. 73, No. 5, March 1968.

Pannekoek, Anton. *Marxism and Darwinism*. Chicago, 1912.

Pilling, Geoffrey, "The Law of Value in Ricardo and Marx." *Economy and Society*, Vol. 1, No. 3, August 1972.

Plamenatz, John. *German Marxism and Russian Communism*. London, 1954.

———. *Man and Society*. Vol. 2, London, 1970.
Plekhanov, Georgi V. *The Development of the Monist View of History*. Moscow, 1972.
———. *Fundamental Problems of Marxism*. New York, 1969.
Poulantzas, Nicos. "On Social Classes," *New Left Review* 78, March–April 1973.
———. *Political Power and Social Classes*. London, 1973.
Roberts, Paul Craig, and Matthew A. Stephenson. *Marx's Theory of Exchange, Alienation, and Crisis*. Stanford, 1973.
Robinson, Joan. *An Essay on Marxian Economics*. London, 1966.
Rosdolsky, Roman. *Zur Enstehungsgeschichte des Marxschen "Kapital."* Frankfurt, 1968.
Rubel, Maximilien. "Reflections on Utopia and Revolution." In Erich Fromm, ed., *Socialist Humanism*. London, 1967.
Sartre, Jean-Paul. *Search for a Method*. New York, 1968.
Schmidt, Alfred. *The Concept of Nature in Marx*. London, 1971.
———. "On the Concept of Knowledge in the Criticism of Political Economy." In *Karl Marx, 1818–1968* (no editor). Bad Godesberg, 1968.
Schumpeter, Joseph A. *Capitalism, Socialism and Democracy*. London, 1954.
Seligman, Edwin. *The Economic Interpretation of History*. New York, 1907.
Sowell, Thomas. "Marx's *Capital* after One Hundred Years." *The Canadian Journal of Economics and Political Science*, Vol. 33, No. 1, February 1967.
———. "Marx's 'Increasing Misery' Doctrine." *American Economic Review*, Vol. 50, No. 1, March 1960.
Stalin, Joseph. *Dialectical and Historical Materialism*. New York, 1940.
Sweezy, Paul. *The Theory of Capitalist Development*. New York, 1968.
Sweezy, Paul, Maurice Dobb, and others. *The Transition from Feudalism to Capitalism: A Symposium*. New York, 1967.
Terray, Emmanuel. *Marxism and "Primitive" Societies*. New York, 1972.
Thorner, Daniel. "Marx on India and the Asiatic Mode of Production." *Contributions to Indian Sociology*, No. 9, December 1966.
Tucker, Robert. *The Marxian Revolutionary Idea*. New York, 1969.
———. *Philosophy and Myth in Karl Marx*. Cambridge, 1961.
Untermann, Ernest. *Marxian Economics*. Chicago, 1913.
Varga, Y. *Politico-Economic Problems of Capitalism*. Moscow, 1968.
Venable, Vernon. *Human Nature: The Marxian View*. Cleveland and New York, 1966.
Weber, Max. "The Social Causes for the Decay of Ancient Civilization." *The Journal of General Education*, Vol. 5, No. 1, October 1950.
Wittfogel, Karl. *Oriental Despotism*. New Haven, 1963.
Witt-Hansen, J. *Historical Materialism: The Method, the Theories*. Copenhagen, 1960.

Wolfson, Murray. *A Reappraisal of Marxian Economics*. Baltimore, 1968.
Yaffe, David S. "The Marxian Theory of Crisis, Capital, and the State."
Economy and Society, Vol. 2, No. 2, May 1973.
Young, Gary. "The Fundamental Contradiction of Capitalist Produc-
tion." *Philosophy and Public Affairs*, Vol. 5, No. 2, Winter 1976.
Zhukov, E. M. "The Periodization of World History." *International
Committee of Historical Sciences, Rapports I*. Stockholm, 1960.

Index

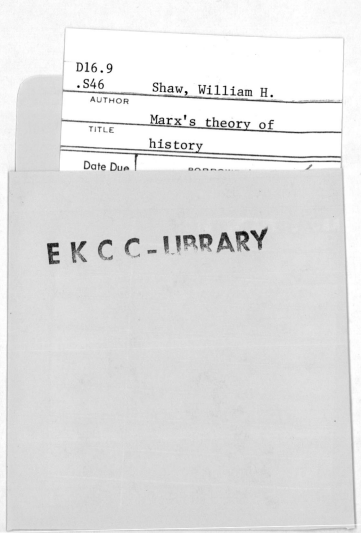